# SUPERDRIVER

**RAC**

# SUPERDRIVER

## Sir John Whitmore

©Fernhurst Books 1988

First published in 1988 for RAC Motoring Services by Fernhurst Books Ltd, 31 Church Road, Hove, East Sussex

ISBN  0 86211 072 6

Printed and bound in Great Britain

**Photo credits**

The photographs on the pages indicated were taken or supplied by the following:
The Central Office of Information: 10, 18, 29
The Ford Motor Company: 17, 21, 38, 49, 51, 52, 56, 58
Haymarket Publishing: Front cover
Saab UK: 3-4
Sir John Whitmore: 7 (both), 9, 24, 30, 31, 33, 37, 39, 40, 41, 50, 54, 57, 59, 61, 62, 63
John Woodward: 19, 23, 27, 44, 46, 60

Design by John Woodward
Composition by A & G Phototypesetting, Knaphill
Artwork by Malcolm Walker
Printed by Ebenezer Baylis & Son Ltd, Worcester

# Contents

# Foreword

I first met John Whitmore in 1964 when he already had the reputation of being one of Britain's best Touring Car drivers. What he did with Minis in racing had become legendary. In published photographs, his cars were invariably travelling sideways with Whitmore grinning at the photographer, and usually laughing at the opposition too!

To race against John, as I had to at times, was always more than a challenge. I know Jim Clark thought the same thing. I was soon to get to know John, not just as a fellow competitor, but as a friend too. Jimmy also was one of John's great friends – in fact he and I shared John's London apartment, which we christened 'The Scottish Embassy'. Later John and I moved to adjacent villages in Switzerland where we spent many an hour in intense conversation.

John's interests expanded into more diverse areas than almost anyone I know, after he retired from racing, but his driving probably remains the thing for which he is best known. His insights into becoming a better driver make fascinating reading. To produce this excellent book, he has also drawn upon his more recent professional experience in mental training, sports psychology and skill development.

To drive well, it is essential to synchronize mind and body to a very high degree and to process all the information gathered by the senses to produce appropriate physical actions. This is not something we are normally taught how to do. John's clear reasoning, and the exercises he suggests, will undoubtedly help drivers to relax, to concentrate better, to drive more smoothly and safely, and to free themselves from the many frustrations that so often arise on the road. In short, this book will show many people the way to becoming super drivers.

I am delighted that John has applied his considerable knowledge of the mind to his old love, driving. After reading this book, it comes as less of a surprise to me that he was recently able to come back winning races again, in spite of having hung up his professional helmet more than twenty years ago! He still knows what he is doing!

**Jackie Stewart**

*The author with Jackie and that other great motorist, Peter Ustinov.*

# 1 The mind matters

Only one thing stops you from becoming the superb driver you always wanted to be. It is not your car, however modest it may be. It is not your passengers, much as they may distract you from the business in hand. And it is certainly not the other drivers, although you may think they are all conspiring against you. No, the real barrier to excellence is you yourself.

Your attention is diverted by your child in the back who drops his ice cream onto the upholstery; a driver pushes in front of you and in a moment of frustration you accelerate to close the gap without noticing that the cars in front are stopping; you see a road sign too late and swerve, narrowly missing an oncoming car. On vacation you find that the hotels are all full, so you decide to drive through the night and become drowsy at the wheel. Back home, unexpected traffic on the daily commute causes you to rush to make up time, and drive beyond your ability, or a wet leaf on the sole of your shoe causes your foot to slip off the brake – with dangerous consequences. These things can, and do, happen to all of us.

Even if no particular incident stands out, we all have days when we would have been better off staying in bed. The car won't start, the jump leads won't make good contact, it begins to rain and you leave for work late, wet and oily – and that was the good bit! Frustration takes over and you seethe. Your mind is driving you to distraction and possibly disaster.

What is happening, and what can you do to avoid such not uncommon experiences?

Whatever the problem, you will generally try to find someone else to blame, or offer some lame explanation to anyone who will listen, for you know it is not like you to get in such a state or make such a mistake. In a way you are right, but the culprit is closer to home than you think. The gremlin who made you act like that lives right inside your own head. This gremlin is your critic and your accuser, your judge and your persecutor. It needs to feel self-important, to be acknowledged, to be right, never to be made a fool of, always to be listened to. It is your ego; it is a part of you, but it is not who you really are.

There are times when the gremlin seems to be asleep. You drive effortlessly. The car feels more responsive than usual, you get the revs just right at every gear change, and you even seem to anticipate the changing patterns in the traffic. Gaps keep appearing in the traffic, so often that you reach your destination several minutes early. Along the way you may have helped other drivers by signalling them into the traffic flow, and got a wave of thanks in return. You arrive feeling alert and alive.

Looking back, the usual chatter of the gremlin was strangely absent. No self-criticism, no frustration with other drivers, no concern about the time and no 'if only. . . ' Your mind seemed to be calm and concentrated, but you may not remember what you were thinking about. You may have no recollection of part of the journey. But you noticed the lightness of your touch on the steering wheel and gearshift, and the undulating note of the engine.

All of us, whatever we do, have experienced these two very different states, and we seem to have very little choice over which state we are in at any particular time. We tend to attribute it to chance or circumstances, and take no responsibility for it ourselves. The former state is 'another of those days'; the latter is a day when 'everything seemed to go right' – it is very pleasurable, but unfortunately more elusive.

This book is mainly about making that state of mind much less elusive. It is about the attitude with which you approach your driving, and it is about how and what you can learn about your skills, your car and yourself that will put the pleasure back into driving.

But before you decide where you are going, you need to know where you are now. What is the reality of the driving condition, and the truth about your own skills and limitations? How much and how often does your gremlin sabotage your ability to drive well, improve and enjoy yourself?

## The driving condition

Driving has truly become a schizophrenic activity. Most small cars come in versions that are capable of well over 100 mph. Many of the larger family models will approach 125 mph, with brakes and handling to match. The top-of-the-range Fords, BMWs and Chevrolets can exceed 150 mph and a 'supercar' like the Ferrari Testarossa can exceed 180. But almost every country now has speed limits of less than 80 mph – and less again off the main highways.

For many drivers the speed limits we are subject to may be welcome since, without them, hooligans in fast cars would be free to scare them and stomp all over them. 'Besides', they would claim, '70 mph is quite fast enough, and what is all the hurry about anyway?' This is a view with which I have some sympathy.

For others, speed limits are a source of frustration and anger. The problem for many drivers, of course, is the differential between the speed limit and the car's potential. Narrow this gap and the temptation and frustration subside. There is a good argument for legislation demanding that manufacturers be prevented from supplying cars capable of more than, say, 90 mph – but it would be sheer heresy in a motoring book to advocate such a sensible solution to the problem.

♦ *A Ferrari Testarossa looks great – but what use is it in a 17-mile tailback?*

## Road accidents are no accident

Road deaths and injuries reached epidemic proportions many years ago. The trend has been slowly downwards in many Western countries during the past 15 years, but the figures remain outrageous. For example, the annual British death toll currently stands at just over 5000 with some 300,000 injuries. In the United States annual road deaths amount to more than 40,000 which is eight times the number of deaths for less than five times the population, although since the mileage per driver is much higher, the number of accidents per mile driven is much the same.

Any other cause of such suffering would be considered quite unacceptable, and governments and health authorities would be forced to act immediately to find both prevention and cure. But the answer is really in our own hands, for it is us, the drivers, who have the power to change things by changing the way we drive. It is incumbent on each of us to ensure that we do not add to the accident statistics, or cause other road users to add to them.

## Your driving

If you are going to change anything – in this case, the way you drive – you need to run a reality check on where you are starting from. If you start from a fantasy, which is either positive or negative, you may never get where you want to go. I invite you to complete the following exercise, simply to raise your own awareness of your starting point.

### Personal reality check

Make several photocopies of this page, fill one in yourself, and ask a few of your regular passengers to fill one in about you to give you their assessment of your driving. Remember that this is simply an opinion that is useful feedback for you. Keep some copies for others to fill in after a few months, and for your first group to fill in again in a year's time.

- How may driving tickets have you accumulated in the past five years?
None . . . . . . 12 or more
- How many parking tickets?
None . . . . . . 12 or more
- How would you describe your driving? Score yourself on a one-to-ten scale, with one representing the quality on the left.
Confident . . . . . . Nervous
Smooth . . . . . . Jerky
Relaxed . . . . . Uptight
Skilful . . . . . . Poor
Fast . . . . . Slow
Safe . . . . . . Dangerous
Patient . . . . . . Impatient

Which of the following apply to you?
- Do you break speed limits?
Seldom. . . . . Regularly
- Driving to meetings, are you ever late?
Never. . . . . . .Usually
- If you are running late, do you suspend your normal road courtesies. . . or phone to say you will be late, and continue driving normally?
- If another driver berates you for an error you made, do you apologize. . . or get angry?
- If you make a mistake, do you signal an apology. . . or attack in defence?

- On a multi-lane highway, do you overtake on the inside lane?
- Do you know approximately how an engine, gearbox, clutch and suspension work?
- Check which three of the following driving conditions give you most concern: ice, fog, driving at night, rain, mountain roads, city traffic, driving abroad, driving an unfamiliar car.
- Are you willing to invest some time in improving your driving?

*This page only is copyright free*

# 2 Taking responsibility

External conditions such as bad weather, bad roads or bad traffic do not cause accidents. There are only two causes of accidents on the road – human failure and mechanical failure.

Mechanical failure accounts for less than five per cent of the total. External factors are ultimately not the problem. They just exist. They do not conspire against us, though we sometimes imagine they do. The real problem is the way you react to those external obstacles. You may not be able to do much about other drivers' reactions, but you can certainly do something about your own.

Keep this distinction clear. You are all too familiar with the external obstacles – the heavy rain, the icy roads, the speed limits, all those trucks, thick fog, pedestrians and, of course, the other driver. You no doubt complain about them constantly; you probably manage to blame them for all the shortcomings in your own driving. But they are not the real problem.

You must recognize and acknowledge the central role played by your own internal reactions: things like impatience, arrogance, lack of concentration or confidence, boredom and, of course, fear. These are the obstacles that really prevent you being the safe, alert, relaxed, confident and unflappable driver you like to imagine you are – but really know you are not.

Such a driver would take whatever conditions he met in his stride, knowing that they are, by and large, beyond his control. By contrast his own response to them is well within his control. It is by taking responsibility for your own reactions that you determine the quality of your personal experience in a car.

▶ *These conditions are not inherently dangerous: they are as dangerous as you make them...*

**Ways and means**
Most road users know how to use the roads properly, but sooner or later some fail to employ that knowledge and cause an accident. This problem cannot be solved by more rigorous conventional driver education alone, or for that matter by more stringent legislation. Merely feeding more 'how-to' information to the intellect is no solution – you already know 'how', but you

don't make use of that knowledge. The secret lies in the less conscious part of the mind which houses your attitudes, your motives and your emotions. It is educating this part of the mind that this book is all about.

So how do you go about it? In the previous chapter I identified some of the *realities* of the *driving condition* and of *our current driving ability*. You now know where the *responsibility* for change lies. The next step is to establish some *goals* for yourself and your driving, and to develop some *motivation* to improve.

In later chapters I will explore the vital importance of raising your *awareness* of all aspects of your driving, identifying the *internal obstacles* that block the way to improvement, and discovering how to eliminate them. The importance of *relaxation* will become apparent, as will the role of *feeling* and *the senses*. I will look at how people *learn* and *develop skills*, and explore the value of *experimentation* in a safe environment.

➥ *Whatever happened to the open road? Gravelly Hill Interchange, Birmingham, England.*

This is a well-tried and logical progression, but even so the ease with which change can take place with minimal effort may surprise you. You may think it won't work. All I can say is – try it!

## Goals

If you want to make a journey, it is important to know where you want to go. So it is with change and with learning. It is essential to know exactly what it is you want to achieve. Presumably you would like to improve your driving and/or enjoy it more, or you would not be reading this book, but improving your driving or enjoying it more is too general. You need to be more specific. How would you really like to drive? With more patience, more smoothly, faster, slower, safer, feeling more relaxed, with better technique? How?

For a goal to be useful, it also has to be realistic and attainable. Many people fall into the trap of setting goals based on myths. For example, there is the myth of the 'open road'. Many drivers like to imagine themselves driving swiftly and stylishly along miles and miles of open country road to the accompaniment of crisp gear changes and a snarling exhaust. In 1934 this might have been a fair aim, but today such an outing is liable to come to grief in a mile-long tailback or a police radar trap.

So what is a realistic goal for your driving? When you drive for pleasure, what is it that you enjoy? When you drive out of necessity, how do you want to spend that time in your car? How do you want to drive? What is it about your driving that you would like to improve?

Some aspects of driving are set by conditions beyond your control; these you can either accept or resist. Others you can determine for yourself. It helps to make choices about both. To make this clearer, imagine you are going to play a game of tennis. The location, the rules and the other players are largely set, and it will help neither your enjoyment nor your performance it you wish you were playing squash. You need to surrender to tennis, and then you can choose how you want to

play it. You can play to win or to have fun; you can play aggressively, stylishly, energetically, or to practise and learn. These choices will be influenced by whether you are a competitor, a pro, a weekend player, or a student of tennis, but the choice is still yours as to how you play the game. You have the same kind of choices when you drive.

Before you turn over the page, try this exercise. You will need a sheet of paper, a pen and about ten minutes. If you are tempted to skip this and read on, please reconsider; some of the value of what follows will be lost if you do.

---

### The ideal driver

Close your eyes and try to imagine the ideal driver. Imagine the driver you would like to be. Now picture yourself in that role. How would you act as such a person? Now go for an imaginary drive, in traffic and on the open road, in colour and on a wide screen. Watch yourself as you drive. Observe how you drive. Imagine the attitudes you would have. Allow yourself sufficient time to develop clear images of a variety of situations: following a slow driver on a narrow road in the rain, or at night, driving over an alpine pass, commuting in a hurry, and so on.

Now take your pen and paper and list, in a column down the left side of the sheet, all the qualities you would possess if you were that ideal driver. Be as wide ranging as you can – patience, alertness, efficiency, perfect eyesight – try to come up with at least 20 such phrases to describe the driver you would like to be.

Now recall being a passenger in the car of the best driver you have ever ridden with. What were the qualities in his or her driving that you most admired? Add them to your list.

What additional qualities would be possessed by someone with acknowledged expertise like a chauffeur, a racing driver or a taxi driver? Write them on your list too.

Now turn the page.

You need to know where you want to go if you are to make a journey, but perhaps even more important is knowing where you are starting from. So it is with learning. You began this process with the exercise at the end of the first chapter. The next part of this exercise will help you discover some more about your driving now, with particular reference to the goal of acquiring some of the qualities you have just listed.

The exercise below will help you clarify the answers to the two fundamental questions: 'What do you want?' and 'What is happening now?' This process will in itself initiate the process of change. Resist the temptation to try to force yourself to become more patient, alert and so on. To do so will almost certainly produce more tension than patience and alertness. Just continue to observe your level of patience and alertness. It is the awareness that produces the change.

## Motivation

Without motivation a goal is nothing more than a dream. Usually we associate motivation with the stick or the carrot with which to beat or tempt the proverbial donkey, and there is no doubt that either, or both, do work some of the time. Neither of them are much fun, however. The stick hurts. The carrot is a short-lived pleasure and it loses its effect once eaten.

It is far more effective, and pleasurable, to acquire a degree of self-motivation. It may be hard to imagine a self-motivated donkey but many people are motivated from within. People engaged in motorsport invariably are. Contrary to popular belief, the money they win is not their driving force. Their need to improve is usually partly a means of overcoming some perceived inadequacy, and partly a matter of aspiration. You may feel the same about your driving.

It is likely that by listing the qualities of the ideal driver, you will have already stirred some motivation. A dynamic tension is set up when you acknowledge the gap between the way you drive now and your ideal. For people with no motivation to drive better, there is no ideal and no gap: there is just driving. It is a chore for them – maybe it is for you too, but can you afford to leave it that way?

How many hours a week do you spend behind the wheel? Fifteen? Twenty-five, perhaps? Are they hours of pain or hours of pleasure? The chances are that those hours will contain a high proportion of frustration, boredom or anxiety.

If you are a moderate road commuter, you will spend some four years of your life in your car. A lot of marriages don't last that long! Apart from in

---

### How do you rate?

On your sheet you now have a long column of ideal qualities. In the next column, rate yourself and the way you usually drive on a scale of one to ten against each of those qualities. For example, if patience was one of the qualities you listed, and you are reasonably patient most of the time, you might rate yourself eight on that.

Add six vertical columns to the sheet so that you can re-rate yourself every week for six weeks. Each time you do it, cover the previous ratings with a ruler so they do not influence the new ones; remember you are rating yourself against an ideal rather than rating your improvement.

As time goes by you may want to add some other qualities to your list. Do so, and rate them too.

Notice, and resist, any temptation to rate yourself higher than you really believe you deserve. The value of this exercise for you will depend upon your honesty with yourself. It is often said that a man will readily admit to being not very good at anything except driving and making love. Women are probably much more honest about both these. You will never have to reveal your rating sheet to anyone so you can afford to be truthful on this occasion!

your home and at your place of work, you will spend more time in the driving seat than in any other single place between leaving school and retiring. If you are a taxi, bus, van or truck driver, a travelling salesman or repairman, your vehicle is also your place of work, and you could be destined to spend one third of your life in it.

Can you afford to spend as much of your life as you do behind the wheel and not do everything you possibly can to improve the quality of your experience?

## Motivation check 1

On a sheet of paper, list all the benefits that you would gain if you were an expert driver. Then, on a second sheet, write down all the resistances you have to becoming an expert.

I have listed some of the more obvious ones below, but write your own lists first, then add any on my list that are true for you.

## Motivation check 2

### Benefits
- I would enjoy driving more.
- I would feel less exhausted after a long drive.
- I would feel safer and more confident.
- I would no longer suffer the discomfort of my nervousness.
- I would enjoy motoring holidays more.
- I could share the driving more.
- I would make some journeys and visits that I avoid making now.
- Perhaps I could get a no-claims bonus.
- My family and friends would have a better time in the car.
- I would feel that I had achieved something.
- I'll show them that women drivers are not so bad.
- I really feel that a man ought to be able drive well, and now I really do.

### Resistances
- I am already an expert, there is nothing he can show me.
- Why waste my time, I am good enough anyway.
- I have not had an accident for years, and the last one was not my fault anyway.
- Accidents are relatively rare, it won't happen to me.
- Relax? Why? I enjoy shouting at other stupid drivers.
- I just can't be bothered.
- I hate driving anyway.
- I'll get around to it someday.
- There's nothing wrong with my driving, I've got a clean licence.
- Don't give me all that psychological claptrap, I am always relaxed. Can't you see that, damn it?

Study your own lists carefully and cross out any that are not particularly important or relevant. Look at what you have left.

Now that you have had your mind focused for a few minutes on your motivation to learn to drive better, and your resistances to doing so, how much motivation are you left with? Rate how motivated you are on a one to ten scale. If you rate above five, read on. It is not really enough, but rate yourself again when you have finished this book. With seven or over you will learn, if you follow the suggestions in the ensuing chapters. If you rate three or less, forget it; you are unlikely to improve much even if you do apply some of the exercises I am going to suggest. Send this book to the best driver you know; she is sure to be interested.

There will always be some people for whom self-motivation to drive better simply does not exist. They are unlikely to respond to the stick or the carrot either. You can inform them of the accident statistics and the causes of accidents, you can threaten them with the law and you can offer them badges of achievement and no-claims insurance bonuses, but they will continue to drive just as badly.

What is needed is a sort of no-claims bonus scheme for good drivers and a penalty for bad ones. We could accumulate good or bad points that would determine the cost of an annually-issued driving licence for the following year. This could go as low as almost nothing, or up to an intimidatingly high sum per year. The money thus collected could be spent directly on safety research, so the worst drivers would be paying for the research. The amount currently spent on road safety research in most countries is extremely low – far less than is spent in researching any disease that kills so many people each year.

It would be even more effective to pay for this licence monthly to remind ourselves how expensive it is to be a bad driver. And wouldn't it be fun if each of us had ten 'good driving' points which we could award each year to other drivers whom we notice doing something particularly considerate. We would be falling over ourselves to help one another!

## SUMMARY

We tend to blame external circumstances on the road for our bad experiences in driving. When we recognize that the problem is often not the external obstacles or other drivers but the way we react to them, we gain the power to change things. We are taking responsibility.

To change the way we drive or the quality of our experience while driving, we need to identify some clearly-defined realizable goals and become fully aware of where we stand now in relation to those goals.

Goals are useless unless we are motivated to achieve them. Prizes and penalties may provide some sort of motivation but the most effective spur to improvement is self-motivation: the drive to excel in whatever we do.

# 3 Awareness and relaxation

Awareness is a word that will appear throughout this book, and since it means different things to different people, it is necessary for me to define what I mean by it.

Awareness is the act of collecting information from your senses. To *raise* your awareness is to gather more detailed and complete information from your senses than normal. To *focus* your awareness is to concentrate your attention on one sense or on one aspect of what is going on.

Awareness is usually concerned with your experience of what is going on in the present as opposed to your thoughts about what went on in the past or your expectations about the future. Implicit in the term awareness is the absence of thought, opinion, criticism, analysis, or judgement about the experience. Awareness gives you unprocessed and unadulterated information.

## Awareness

Wherever you are sitting reading this book right now, be it unwisely in your car in a traffic jam on the highway, furtively at your office desk or dozily in bed, here is an exercise to illustrate what I mean when I use the term awareness.

Place your attention on the points of contact between you and the seat which supports you. What does the pressure feel like? Where exactly on your body are those points, how hard is the pressure, what is the relative firmness of that pressure on your bottom, your back, and on your feet? Now move, and note how those feelings shift.

Unless you are in a car, close your eyes and you may be able to feel more, as this will eliminate the dominant visual sense on which we are normally so dependent. Your tactile sense 'expands' to fill the gap and make up for the lack of vision.

Now check through your body inside your skin, starting with your toes. Notice any feelings of warmth or coolness, tension or tiredness. Notice what you feel in each part of your body. Don't judge it, don't analyse it, just experience it.

Now move a little and notice how the experience of different parts of your body changes. Experience and enjoy those feelings in the same passive way as you would hear and enjoy the sounds of a piece of music: one phrase after another, non-judgementally.

There are two forms of awareness: the first involves being aware of things outside your body, while the second is an awareness of what is going on inside. Athletes and dancers develop a high degree of sensitivity to the insides of their bodies. Not unexpectedly they call it 'listening to the body'. Masseurs and sculptors have a highly developed sense of touch. Generally sensitivity and skill develop in parallel, so excelling at a sport will make you more sensitive. More importantly for our purposes, if you develop your sensitivity, you will become more skilful at what you do: you will become a better athlete, dancer, sculptor – or driver.

## Driving awareness

The last awareness exercise showed you what the process of being non-judgementally aware really means, and what it feels like. Now do the same thing while you are driving. To begin with, try it for short periods at a time.

As you are driving, focus on the pressure points between you and the seat, your hands and the wheel, your feet and the pedals when you push them. Notice the sensations and feel them changing.

Check inside your body also. Notice any tightness, tiredness or discomfort in your muscles. Don't try to do anything about it, just register it in as much detail as you can. What exactly is the sensation? Where exactly in your body do you experience it? When does it occur as you drive? All the time, or only when the traffic is heavy, for example? How strong is the sensation? Call it five as it is now, on a one to ten scale, and notice if it increases or decreases as you watch it. Keep rating it on that scale for a while.

You will find that as you maintain your focus upon it, the numbers will decrease and the discomfort will dissolve. You may find yourself altering your position in the seat or even wanting to move the seat. Go ahead and do it – your body is telling you what it wants and, like an athlete, you are now listening to your body.

---

The act of placing a high degree of awareness on some aspect of yourself and your driving will automatically result in improvement, whether it is a relaxation of tension, which in itself enhances learning, or the refining of a driving skill.

If you are too anxious to get a result from this process, however, you will be focused on the result instead of merely observing what is happening, and the process will not work for you. The paradox is that results come from the focused observation, not from trying to change anything.

Doing the awareness exercise from time to time as you drive will help you to be more relaxed and comfortable, and as you develop increased sensitivity you will begin to notice and change small but important things about the way you drive. A person who drives a reasonable mileage with a high level of awareness will learn and improve far more than a person who covers a very high mileage without much awareness.

We will be exploring two aspects of driving awareness. The first has to do with what goes on inside the car. This includes what happens inside the driver's mind in terms of attitude, and what happens inside the driver's body in terms of relaxation. It also includes the smooth and efficient use of the controls. The second aspect of driving awareness has to do with the external conditions such as the road geography, surfaces, weather and, of course, other road users.

We will be looking in more depth at the use of car controls and at observation outside the car in a later section dealing with skill development. Here we are going to look at what goes on in a driver's mind – or what does not!

Inattention is probably the single most common cause of road accidents. We have all heard, or used, the expression 'I just did not see the car coming'. We all know that if we pay attention, we are far less likely to have an accident, but merely knowing that is not enough. So what causes our attention to wander and where does it go?

## Internal obstacles

Clearly when we are engaged in any activity we have appropriate thoughts, such as paying attention to the job in hand, and we have other thoughts which can detract from our efficiency, enjoyment and performance. These 'other thoughts' could be described as internal obstacles

since they get in the way of the smooth, efficient mental processes that enable us to perform well. They include emotions, such as anger, and body sensations, such as tension.

An example of this is the pressure to perform well. When someone says to me, 'I suppose I should let you drive' as they strap themselves firmly into the driving seat, I know I am in for a rough ride. To suffer the attempts of others to show off their driving prowess is a painful experience that racing drivers often have to bear. It usually takes the form of a jerky, stomach-turning jaunt to the tune of squealing tyres and crunching gears. The lyrics are muttered abuse aimed at other road users and the plaintive excuses of the usually perfectly reasonable driver who cannot understand why his driving ability has suddenly deserted him.

Such awful attempts to drive as someone imagines a racing driver would drive are not uncommon; they are embarrassing at best and disastrous at worst. You may not have experienced being pressured by having an expert driver as a passenger, but you will probably have had a closely-related experience at some time in your life. So when it happens, what is really going on? The self-created pressure to perform has become an obstacle to the smooth mental efficiency that enables you to drive well. You are no longer driving: you are being driven, by your ego and your anxiety, and the harder you try the worse it gets.

## Internal obstacles

Take a sheet of paper and divide it into four columns as illustrated here. In the first column write down all the internal obstacles that you experience from time to time. In the second column give them a rating (on a one-to-ten scale) according to how much and how often you experience them. In the third column write down the particular conditions that you associate them with. Rate the significance of their impact upon your driving in the fourth column on the one-to-ten scale. It might begin something like this:

| Internal Obstacles | Rating | Associated Conditions | Rating |
|---|---|---|---|
| Frustration | 6 | Police | 7 |
| | | Speed limits | 4 |
| | | Heavy traffic | 3 |
| Anxiety | 4 | Night driving | 3 |
| | | Icy roads | 6 |

Here are some more of the most common internal obstacles which, if they are true for you, you might like to add to your list.

**Fear**

If you avoid driving on a particular road because you are afraid of fast-moving traffic you will have put down 'fear' in the first column of your list, and you might have put down 'fast-moving traffic' in the third.

Think about this for a moment. Your full inner statement might go something like this: 'I am afraid of being hit by a fast-moving truck whose driver cannot stop or has not seen me'.

As is usually the case, the external obstacle – the truck – is not really the problem at all. Most are well driven and most remain within the speed limit, and those that are not are beyond your control. The real problem, and the one you *can* do something about, is your fear, which detracts from

your enjoyment of driving and, worse still, causes you to lose confidence. We all know that when we lack confidence, we are most likely to make a mistake.

In your case it may go like this. On the highway you are approaching several trucks, or worse they are approaching you from behind. You begin to get nervous and lift off the accelerator, or actually stab at the brake. You may even erratically change lanes to get as far away from them as possible. Your unexpected manoeuvre may cause a truck to swerve, to pass too close or to honk loudly at you. This will all serve to reinforce your belief that trucks, truck drivers and probably multi-lane highways are all dangerous. Your fear of each will increase, and so the vicious cycle builds.

You may think this example is exaggerated, but it certainly is not for some people. Besides, can you honestly say that you yourself are not subject to similar fears about some situations? Maybe you had a little skid once on a wet road that resulted in a minor accident. What happened? You no longer enjoy driving whenever it is wet, and when you *have* to drive in the wet, you are tentative, reactive and therefore less safe. And so it goes.

## Myth and reality
You have now constructed a myth that trucks or wet roads are far more dangerous than they really are, and you continue to react to the myth rather than the reality.

Some myths like the ones in our example are self-created, but others stem from conventional wisdom – or rather the lack of it. For example, many drivers fail to swerve to avoid an accident, or fail to wrench the wheel around if they are suddenly confronted with a sharper corner than they expected. Instead, they brake too hard, lock the front wheels and so lose all steering effect, and plough straight on.

In part this is caused by the instinctive reaction to slow down at all costs, but it also stems from the conditioned myth that a car will turn over if it is turned sharply at high speed. The fact is that a modern car won't, unless it hits something pretty substantial.

## Being right
Oh no, this is not you. You would not make such an error. Nothing bothers you. You are supremely confident at all times. Nonsense! You are either not telling the truth or you lack self-awareness.

Yes, you guessed it. One big internal obstacle, especially prevalent among male drivers, is believing that they are always right, and therefore that the other person is always to blame for any inconvenience or incident. For the worst of these drivers, the mere existence of other road users makes them an enemy to be scorned and defeated.

I dare you to write this one down in the first column of your list of internal obstacles.

## Anxiety
Anxiety in a driver may arise out of an immediate situation, such as heavy traffic causing you to worry about being late for an important appointment. It may surface every time you step into your car because you are afraid of having an accident, or it may only become a problem when one of your children is in the car. Many people are chronically anxious or stressed about issues which have nothing to do with their driving, but affect it nevertheless. Regardless of the root cause, stress, tension and anxiety seriously impair the performance, safety and pleasure of driving.

## Anxiety and stress

Let us look first at the anxiety that arises specifically from driving. On a sheet of paper, make up a table like the one below. As in the examples I have given, write down all the things you are afraid of, or get angry about, at different times while driving – being late for work, having an accident on a notorious stretch of road, the kids getting hurt, hitting cyclists or motorcyclists, scratching your new car, drivers who overtake and push in, big trucks, blowouts at speed, police officers and speed limits, and so on.

Opposite each issue write down the effects that it has upon you when it arises, in terms of thoughts, emotions and body sensations. In the next column describe the way you usually react under these circumstances. To do this accurately you should recall some specific incidents you have had on the road; perhaps take a recent example of each and rerun it through your mind's eye as vividly as you can. You will be surprised at how clearly the thoughts and feelings return.

While the incident is fresh in your mind, take a moment to imagine yourself as the supremely calm, confident and relaxed driver you would like to be. How would you have handled the incident then? What would you have done? How would you have felt?

Now write down in the Action column the things you are willing to do differently next time such circumstances arise. Vague things like 'Be more courteous' or 'Leave home a little earlier' are too general. Be more specific. How are you going to be more courteous? How much earlier are you going to leave?

| Anxiety | Effect | Behaviour | Action |
|---|---|---|---|
| Being late for work | Impatience and anger with other drivers | Risk-taking and lack of consideration | Leave home 15 minutes earlier each morning |
| | Tension, fatigue | Erratic driving and poor judgement | keep observing the tension level in my body as I drive for a week |

What you are doing in the anxiety exercise is trying yet again to find the answers to those two crucial questions 'What happens?' and 'How do I want to be?' These questions are fundamental. Change is unlikely to occur until you are very clear about what you feel and do, and very clear about what you want to move towards. Then it begins automatically. Change invariably occurs this way, although conventional wisdom would have it that nothing is achieved without striving. This is simply not true. Motivation, yes, but striving to change yourself and your behaviour only produces more anxiety, guilt and fear of failure.

## Tension

Tension may also be alleviated at the purely physical level without seeking the underlying cause. Relief is often only partial or temporary, but it may be total and permanent. Again you apply the principle of becoming clear about precisely what is occurring, but this time on the physical level, and becoming clear about what you want, which is obviously to feel relaxed. Change for the better will begin to take place almost at once.

Try the exercise below. If you consciously use this technique every ten minutes or so for a few days while you are driving you will soon find you can do it very quickly; before long, a regular check on your tension will be as easy as a glance at the fuel gauge. Notice that it is not a case of forcing yourself to relax, which is a contradiction in terms. By merely becoming aware of your tensions and focusing your attention on the sensations in some detail, they will be reduced. Do not analyse, judge, criticize yourself or develop a lot of opinions about your tension. Just experience the various sensations, rather as you would listen to a piece of music.

### Relieving tension

While you are driving, check through your body from head to toe to see if you are experiencing tension.

If you are, you need to find out exactly what the body sensations are, when they occur, where in the body they are located, and how strong they are. Check your facial, neck and shoulder muscles. Is your grip on the wheel too tight? As you monitor the sensations, they may move and alter in form, but almost certainly they will begin to dissolve. When you are monitoring tension it may be useful to grade it on a one-to-ten scale, with five being the starting level. The figure may rise briefly as you become aware of the extent of the tension, but it will soon fall again.

### More internal obstacles

The list of possible internal obstacles is endless. There is perfectionism, trying too hard to do it right, impatience, and competitiveness. All these stem from self-doubt, and result in physical tension which causes discomfort and detracts from your driving performance and your enjoyment of driving.

Other kinds of internal obstacle include laziness, disinterest, lack of consideration for others, lapses in concentration and poor observation: all forms of inattention. I imagine that you will have found others that I have not listed, but most will fall into either the self-doubt or the inattention category, and some may well fit into both.

So now you have a long list of your own internal obstacles to safe and enjoyable driving, and a number of other potential ones that I have mentioned. Now what?

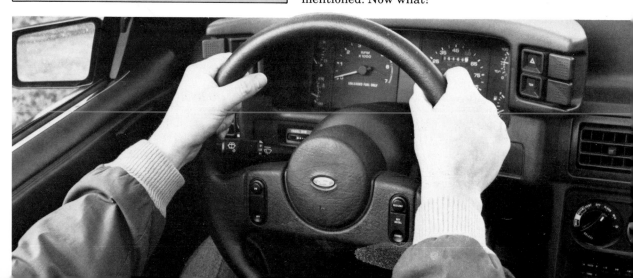

### Eliminating the internal obstacles

Congratulations, you are already some of the way towards doing just that. For many people, recognizing and acknowledging their weaknesses and the effects they have upon their driving, as you have done by listing them, is very difficult. It is also an important first step towards change.

You might find yourself tempted to say, 'I am not going to get irritated any more when I am overtaken'. This is very commendable, but it won't work. Oh yes, you can button your lip or even force a smile. You can change your behaviour with an act of will – so long as you remember to. At least that is better than hurling epithets around the inside of the car like you usually do. Or is it?

At least by yelling you release some of the emotional charge. The usual alternative is that you repress your emotions and fight down the effects of the adrenalin rush in your solar plexus and upper arm muscles. You develop a vice-like grip on the wheel and your attention will certainly not be on what you are doing. At this point another driver notices your erratic behaviour and hoots at you to get you back on track. Now you get mad at him, and at yourself for falling into your own trap, and so it goes. An exaggeration, perhaps – but I'll bet it has a ring of truth, too.

Trying hard to behave differently seldom produces the results we would like. Besides, it is our propensity for irritation that we want to change, not just our outward behaviour.

If the elimination of our negative attitudes or internal obstacles is so crucial to good driving, why is it that the subject is not to be found anywhere in the current driving school curriculum? This sort of education, so vital to every road user for his or her own survival, is actually very hard to come by. Why? It is because, while most people are willing to learn a new skill, they regard tampering with attitudes and emotions as impossible ('This is just how I am'), unnecessary ('There is nothing wrong with me') or dangerous ('I am not going to let anyone mess with my head'). In fact it is quite possible, very necessary if we are to reduce our accident rate, and anything but dangerous.

# L.A. violence turns freewa into war zone

## 'I wonder if the guy riding next to me has a gun . . .' Will he 'kill me?'

LOS ANGELES — A dea string of freeway shootir has millions of Southern C fornia commuters feeling li moving targets — and the r of the country fearing the v lence could spread.

Four people have be killed and several injured ir rash of armed violence in the fast lane building here sin June. The latest two deaths came Sunday, but drivers a riders in the estimated 250,000 cars choking the hundre of miles of highways lacing this metropolis during an ave age day's rush hour are waiting for the next bullet to hit

"What we have is a war out there," says psychiatrist I Ange Lobue, of College Hospital in Cerritos.

Experts say the series of nine shootings among motoris emerged from a reservoir of pent-up rage common to tho who spend hours trapped behind the wheel on anonymou gray strips of road. Occasional incidents of warring dr vers going for their guns have been r in rec

's shooti

It is also very simple to understand, if a little hard to believe. The secret of change lies in knowing precisely what we want and what is happening now. When we are clear about these two things, change will take place without having to resort to force and effort.

Of course this is hard to accept, brought up as we were from the cradle to believe that nothing is worth having unless we work hard for it. The concept of change without effort is quite foreign to most of us, but it works nonetheless.

## In two minds

Another way of looking at the problem of internal obstacles is to imagine that the mind is divided into two parts: the natural mind and the anxious mind. Of course this is an oversimplification, but it is an idea that can serve us well.

If you think you need to have your intellectual, analytical faculties constantly in gear to drive well, you are mistaken. You can walk, run, cycle, brush your teeth and do a whole host of other complex tasks without giving them much thought. Indeed you can do all these things equally well when you are thinking about something quite different, and you rarely, if ever, instruct or criticize yourself about the way you do them.

The part of your mind that manages to do these things so well, I call the natural mind. The part of your mind that judges, criticizes, instructs, gets nervous, worries and does not trust the natural ability of the natural mind, I call the anxious mind. Most of us have experienced the shrill monologue of the anxious mind while we have been attempting to master a new skill. It went

*◆ Faraway thoughts: perfect balance – you don't need your intellect to tell you how to ride a bike, so are you sure you need it to drive well?*

something like this during that driving test that you failed!

'You will never make the three-point turn on a road with as much camber as this. . . You didn't signal early enough. . . Get the wheel over quickly, and don't roll into the curb. . . That was lucky, but you will never be so lucky in reverse. . . Stop, stop. There you go, idiot, I told you so. He is bound to fail you now. . .'

With all this going on you utterly failed to see the halt sign and it was that – not the three point turn – that led to your failure. Recognize it? In its concern, your anxious mind sabotaged your natural mind, which was not doing a bad job until that happened.

Now let us look at the other end of the spectrum. Think of something you do really well; maybe a sport, something at work, or even some aspect of driving. Try to recall an incident when you performed particularly well. I'll bet that on that occasion, the doing of it was very natural and fluid, there was no chatter at all from your anxious mind, and you felt relaxed.

The sooner and the more you trust your natural mind to get on with the job in hand, the better. As you gain experience and confidence in your ability to master a skill such as driving, you become increasingly able to let your natural mind take over the management of the basics. This allows you to give some attention to the refinement of your driving skills, and I will look at that in detail in later chapters.

## Relaxation

Trusting the natural mind is largely a matter of relaxation. We all know that relaxation is a beneficial state, one in which you feel good and perform well, but few of us have ever been taught how to relax. Few people can relax on demand; in fact telling someone to relax will, at best, evoke a brief letting-go, and will often cause more tension. Relaxation is not an active state that can be turned on at will. It is our natural passive state which can be disrupted by the anxieties and fears which I have described as internal obstacles.

Relaxation occurs when you experience a temporary absence of internal obstacles or when you are operating under the control of your natural mind. In your daily life you move in and out of this state as the degree of internal interference you experience varies. If you practise maintaining your awareness when you drive, you will be relaxed for more of the time, and drive better, too.

A good driver will always appear relaxed at the wheel. He or she will sit back in the driver's seat with both hands holding the steering wheel firmly but lightly at approximately the 'ten-minutes-to-two' position. His or her movements over the controls will be minimal, fluid, unhurried and purposeful. The calm confidence exuded by such a driver will also be conveyed to the passengers.

◆ *Relaxation at the wheel: driving sideways at speed in a racing Mini Cooper of the '60s, the author still finds time for a traditional salute to the photographer.*

These are the observable characteristics of a driver who is relaxed. To emulate the posture and movements of a relaxed driver will not in itself make you into one, for relaxation comes from the inside out, not the outside in, but playing the role of being relaxed can help to evoke it.

Another most effective aid to relaxation while driving is to listen to music. The choice of music will obviously depend on your taste but do not be surprised if some kinds of music help you to relax much better than others.

I taught skiing for several years using a method known as the Inner Game. Rather than giving my students a lot of technical instructions which often confuse and frustrate, my goal was to calm or divert the anxious mind which so inhibits learning, performance and enjoyment, and to encourage the natural learner, or skier, to emerge. Music played on a personal stereo was one of the most effective tools I used. Not infrequently the relaxation it created resulted in quite dramatic improvements in skiing with no technical input at all. So it can be with driving.

What music does, of course, is to divert our attention from the tension-creating concerns that tend to course through our minds. It holds the mind still and soothes it. If your concerns are driving-related, they will be calmed too.

## Driving in automatic

At times many drivers experience the sudden realization that they have no recall whatsoever of the past twenty miles of their journey. It is a strange and interesting phenomenon, but a little disconcerting because one never knows how well or badly one drove.

Almost certainly, if you have had such an experience, you drove as well, if not better than you usually do. The reason is that your natural mind was taking care of the driving while your anxious mind was focused elsewhere. You were driving in the mental state in which you normally walk. Your anxious mind was not interfering with the ability of your natural mind, and your body was relaxed and operating at peak efficiency. I am not suggesting that you should try to get into this state – the act of trying would make it impossible anyway – but if you create the conditions for relaxed driving you may find yourself driving in automatic from time to time.

Diverting the anxious mind away from worrying about driving undoubtedly improves driving in many instances. Unfortunately it is hard for an already nervous driver to be sure that taking his attention away from his driving will not make things worse. He already feels that his mind is unable to cope adequately with all the things he believes he has to think of to drive safely, and the deliberate introduction of some sort of distraction would seem like the formula for disaster. In fact, as I have pointed out already, what we are trying to divert is not the part of the mind that does the driving but the anxious, critical, chattering voice in the head that does not trust the driving part, takes it over and causes you to make mistakes.

## SUMMARY

Awareness is information-gathering through the senses rather than through the intellect. It is the key to change and improvement which occurs automatically as awareness is raised in the area to be changed.

As you do this one of the things you are likely to become aware of is the variety of internal obstacles, such as anger and anxiety, that interfere with your performance and your enjoyment of driving.

We appear to have two minds: the anxious mind which is filled with concerns, criticisms and instructions, and the natural mind which seems to be in charge when we are doing things well and enjoying ourselves.

As you raise your awareness of your own internal obstacles as they arise, they will be reduced; you become more relaxed, and you begin to act more from your natural mind.

# 4 Changing conditions

We have looked at some of the internal obstacles that arise while driving in the 'normal' condition. By this I mean in the daytime, in reasonable visibility, on normal road surfaces in your own car or at least in a familiar car, and without undue interferences of any kind. Any changes in your driving or any experimentation should be tried out first in these familiar conditions.

When you drive in unfamiliar conditions or conditions that are considered to be less safe, your anxieties and other internal obstacles are likely to reappear. In this chapter I will discuss a number of these external conditions to make you more aware of some of the factors associated with them. The basis of much anxiety is an underlying fear of the unknown. As the conditions become more of a known quantity, the fear subsides and the anxiety tends to recede.

The intellectual information supplied here is incomplete and it is no substitute for gaining experience by *choosing* to drive in those conditions. Many people avoid the external conditions they do not like and therefore deny themselves the opportunity of overcoming their limitations. This is all very well, but sooner or later they are caught out, and find that they can't cope. Next time the weather closes in, get the car out and go for a drive! You may learn something.

## Night driving

When we drive we depend very heavily on sight, and much of the information we use by day is no longer available to us at night. Inevitably we are forced to rely a little more on assumptions. Driving at night does, therefore, introduce extra anxieties for many people.

Most of us outgrow the more obvious manifestations of our childhood fears of the dark, but for many those fears continue to lurk in their subconscious. Perhaps the most prevalent of all human fears is the fear of the unknown. We are so sight-dependent, especially when we drive, that we tend to believe that that which we cannot see, we cannot know.

To overcome this problem when driving at night you have to trust your assumptions and your experience. For example, although you cannot see the road beyond the limits of the headlights, you have to assume that it continues. And although you often cannot see the road surface very well at night, it probably does not differ much from other surfaces you have experienced.

Trusting to your assumptions becomes more tricky if you assume that those dark areas which the headlights do not penetrate are always unoccupied. On certain roads cyclists or pedestrians with dark clothes and no lights are taking great risks that they may be quite unaware of, if they are not car drivers, and a couple of near misses can completely undermine a driver's confidence. The answer is to cultivate a higher level of awareness, and take account of all the little indicators that you can see. Two factors mitigate against you, however. The first is the likelihood of being tired, which will limit awareness, and second problem is that eyesight which is adequate in the day may be far from sufficient to perceive the subtle signs at night – especially if you wear glasses.

At night it is vital to keep your windscreen clean, and if this means stopping every now and again, so be it. You need all the visibility you can get; oncoming headlights on a dirty screen will put you and others at grave risk.

◆ *Street lights, reflections, glare – all the hazards of the night can add up to confusion and possible disaster. But need they?*

You have to watch the other drivers too. Since people drink more at night, can see less at night, have more anxieties at night and may be more sleepy at night, the drivers you encounter along the way are likely to be more erratic than they are in daylight, even if you are not.

One of my wife's greatest fears of driving at night, and she is certainly not alone in this, is getting lost. Sadly in many places a woman who is lost or who has a breakdown may very reasonably be afraid of asking for help. As a teenager in America, my wife once crashed into the back of a car which had broken down in the fast lane of a freeway at night, and which had no lights on.

Injured and bleeding, she was then taken hostage for fifteen minutes by a madman with a knife who appeared from out of the night and wanted to protect her from the ambulance men!

And if I have not put you off driving at night for ever, remember that fog, frost and ice are far more likely to form at night, as well.

**Asleep at the wheel**
Some of the most serious accidents occur at night as a result of drivers falling asleep at the wheel. Not only are you more likely to be tired at night, but moving lights, particularly if they happen to fall into certain frequencies, do have a mesmerizing effect. The warning signs are the fixed stare, the sensation of driving down a tunnel formed by the light of your headlights, yawning and, less commonly known, a tendency to touch

your face or the back of your neck. By the time the car is wandering or your head is dropping at regular intervals, you are in the last stages before the crash.

There is only one answer and that is STOP. Pull off the road and go to sleep for a while in the car. The next hotel may be too far away. Do not risk it. Drinking strong black coffee, despite its awful health implications, will help some people though it takes some while to take effect. I have tried turning the radio up, turning it off, turning the heater off, opening the windows, talking to myself and getting someone to talk to me. They all help, sometimes, for a short while.

If they don't help, then stop you must. The inconvenience is far outweighed by the risks of carrying on. Most of those who died, and who killed others, by falling asleep at the wheel, either did not recognize they were at risk or thought they could make it. They didn't. Don't join them.

---

### Night driving

Take a sheet of paper and list the aspects of night driving that worry you most, drawing upon your own experience and on the points that I have raised. Rate each of them on a one to five scale according to how much they affect you. By identifying the problems in this way, you are already part of the way towards eliminating your fears.

---

### Wet roads

Modern radial-ply tyres, correctly inflated, give excellent adhesion in the wet most of the time. But mud, oil slicks or worn road surfaces can create slippery patches which may catch you out. For this reason some cornering speed reduction and more gentle use of accelerator and brakes is called for.

If you lock the brakes or enter a corner too fast you may go into a front-wheel skid. This will take the form of a loss of steering effect and a tendency

to plough straight ahead. The appropriate response is to reduce the pressure on the brake or accelerator pedal, whichever has caused the problem, and avoid vigorous use of the steering wheel or brakes until adhesion has been regained.

A rear wheel skid will generally occur further into a corner than a front wheel skid, but again it is usually caused by harsh use of the accelerator or brake in slippery conditions. The car will appear to turn more sharply than you intended and you will have to quickly reduce the steering lock, and even turn onto the opposite lock if necessary. But while this is the logical and natural response, such a skid will invariably catch out a driver who has not experienced one before, and it takes practice to develop the skill to cope with a rear wheel skid without concern. Disengaging the clutch in either type of skid may help the wheels regain adhesion more quickly.

While I have described some actions to take if your car skids, there is no substitute for trying it out. A session on a skid pan will give you valuable experience of what it feels like, and will help to reduce your anxiety about skidding.

### Ice and snow

What I have said about skidding on wet roads applies in icy and snowy conditions, except that on ice and snow the skid will occur at a much slower speed. You will have more time to respond, but the stopping distances, particularly on ice, are far longer than most drivers think.

In addition, some types of ice are very hard to detect when concealed by wet surfaces at night, and you should always be cautious when freezing point approaches. Snow can soon become rutted and the ruts themselves can have the effect of both holding the car on line and throwing it off line unexpectedly, so be careful.

Slippery conditions, however they are caused, are likely to provoke anxiety in the mind, and tension in the hands and arms. This is just what you don't want because a light grip and the sensitivity to 'feel' the constantly changing

are therefore beyond the reach of the average motorist. Skid pans provide an opportunity to learn how to control a skid once it has begun, but since the skid is predictable you learn little about responding quickly and appropriately to an unexpected loss of control on the road. Both are time-consuming and demand special locations which are few and far between. Many drivers, and probably those who would benefit most from them, would not dream of attending either for fear of accident and injury, or of making a fool of themselves – although both fears are unjustified.

Help is at hand, however. A car has recently been developed that uses four-wheel-steering under sophisticated electronic control to simulate all kinds of skidding situations at very low speeds, and at the touch of a button. The system's inventors claim that it is the most significant practical breakthrough in driver training since the introduction of the driving test. This is quite a claim, but after spending a half hour behind the wheel of the prototype just before going to press, I was very impressed by its potential. Here is why.

The realism of the skid simulation, even on the prototype, is quite uncanny, and I speak as a racing driver with a reputation for a spectacular driving style in which the car was rarely pointing in the direction in which it was going!

The types of apparent skid that can be induced and the speed of response required are instantly and infinitely variable from the driver or passenger seat. This means that it can be set up to suit any existing skill level from that of a learner to that of a Grand Prix driver.

The device is effective at any car speed down to a walking pace, enabling it to be used anywhere from a racing circuit to a school yard or car park with complete safety.

The car can be used to simulate the different types of skids that characterize front or rear-wheel-drive cars and it can be used to provide a replicable and quantifiable test of a driver's real car control ability. It lends itself particularly well to the more recent, more enjoyable and more effective student-centered learning methods advocated throughout this book.

slipperiness is what you need. To drive safely on slippery surfaces it is essential to be relaxed – but the confidence that will enable you to relax only comes with experience and awareness.

Unfortunately such experience is only available to competition drivers who have been at the game for some years. Racing driver schools and skid pans, both of which I recommend, are useful substitutes but both have severe limitations.

Racing driver schools are expensive, particularly if you spend enough time at one for the correct responses to become automatic. They

It can enable every driver to experience what happens in an emergency when a car reaches the limits of adhesion. Even if some people have difficulty controlling the 'skid', at least they will have penetrated the dark void of 'the unknown beyond' that haunts so many anxious drivers.

Finally, and most importantly, a car so equipped is enormous fun to play around with and learn from. If this statement seems to run counter to the serious business of teaching people to drive more safely, let me assure you that it is not. Our usable recall of pleasant experiences is far greater than our recall of unpleasant ones, which we tend to block: although we continue to feel the painful emotions associated with unpleasant experiences, we often deny ourselves the value of learning from them. The enormous enjoyment to be derived from driving the skid simulator ensures optimum learning from the experience.

It is obvious that this device has immense potential for driver education at all levels. It has made skid pans obsolete overnight and can make car control training available to every driver. This is why I too believe that this may be the most important contribution to driver education since the introduction of the driving test.

## Skidding

Is skidding an issue for you? Note down the conditions and the aspects of skidding with which you feel least able to cope. Rate your level of concern about each of them on a one to five scale. Once again, identifying your problems will help reduce your level of anxiety.

## Getting stuck

In mud, snow or on ice, it is not difficult to get stuck, especially on a hill. There are two ways to get up the slippery slope. One is to take a run at it, while the other involves very gentle use of the clutch and accelerator to minimize the spinning of the wheels. Rocking the car back and forth between first and reverse gears may help you to get out of a rut, and even one person pushing, while the driver attempts to drive out, can make a surprising difference. (If you have a front-wheel-drive car it may help to turn round and go up backwards. This puts the weight of the car where you need it, over the driving wheels.)

It is also easy to get stuck in water but for different reasons; when the water reaches the engine it is likely to cut. Despite this it is quite possible to cross a section of road flooded with water up to a foot (30cm) deep, if you know what you are doing. The trick is to keep the engine speed up and the car speed down. The slow car speed prevents a bow wave building up which could drown the electrics. The high engine speed stops the water from entering the exhaust pipe and killing the engine. First gear is not nearly slow enough in deep water, and it will be necessary to keep the clutch slipping.

In an automatic car select the low gear hold, keep some pressure on the brake with the left foot

◀ *In an alpine ski resort snow is taken for granted, and some drivers actually enjoy it.*

to keep the car speed down, and keep the engine speed up with the throttle.

A few more words of warning: do not attempt to cross a fast-moving stream, even if it is only a foot deep. And if you have no idea how deep the flood is, or how strong the flow is, walk across it first. It is better to suffer wet feet than find yourself stranded with a dead engine.

After crossing water, drive slowly for a short distance keeping your left foot firmly on the brakes to clear them of water, then check them to ensure that they are working.

## Fog and bad visibility

Most people drive too fast for the visibility and their own ability in fog and other poor conditions. Awareness is once again the secret. You should continuously monitor your speed in relation to how far you can see, because the thickness of fog frequently varies. If weather conditions during the day suggest an evening fog, try to arrange to complete your journey before dark, because visibility in fog is dramatically reduced by darkness. Use dipped headlamps day and night and use your bright rear lights. Your point of visual focus should be as far as you can see up the edge of the road on your side; most important of all, look at what you *can* see rather than strain your eyes into the murk where you can't see anything. Eye strain in fog or driving snow can quickly turn to drowsiness.

Bad visibility outside is one thing, but some people compound the problem by not keeping all the car windows as clean and mist-free as possible. When there is fog outside, you may not notice the mist building up on the inside or the outside of the windscreen. Keep a rubber squeegee and scraper in the car at all times, and use it before you drive off to clear dew, ice and snow from every window.

I was a passenger in a police car not so long ago, when we stopped a driver suspected of being drunk due to his erratic progress down the road. He was not drunk; he was peering through a four-inch diameter clear spot in a windscreen otherwise completely obscured by ice. His folly deserved the penalty he would have received had he been drunk. He was every bit as dangerous.

☛ *Keep a clear screen – and a clear head – when the weather closes in.*

## Driving in foreign countries

Driving in a foreign country presents us with a string of unfamiliar situations that may seem daunting at first. The problems are more in the mind than in reality, but for some people they are very real and they start to arise some weeks before departure. Many of the common concerns are not even directly related to driving, but nevertheless they warrant attention here because they inevitably affect the pleasure and the safety of the drive.

Can we drink the water? Will I be able to find my way? What will the hotel or campsite be like? Will they be able to speak English, and how will I be able to make myself understood if they don't? What if the children get sick? What am I going to forget? What if I have car trouble? Is Aunt Emily going to be able to cope while we are away? Did I get all the paperwork that we need? And so it goes.

The list of possible concerns is endless. Some of these may seem silly to you, but we all have our own versions of this list, and the touchiness that one observes at ports and airports suggests that the arousal level of many travellers runs much too high for comfort. What is more, the anxiety generated is often vented on the kids in the back or all those foreigners, none of whom are responsible for our neurosis.

As can be seen from the exercise below, many common concerns can be reduced or eliminated by seeing the reality of the situation instead of surrendering to catastrophic fantasies, and if necessary taking some specific course of action ahead of time.

Most countries have excellent national automobile associations that can help to relieve the concerns. For example the RAC in England and AAA in the United States offer a variety of goods and services for just this purpose, from jump leads and tow ropes to ferry reservations, personal insurance and car recovery plans. The proportion of your total holiday cost that these services represent is very small indeed, especially if they are regarded in the light of what a health problem or car recovery might cost if it happens to you – which it never will, unless it does!

Once you have taken specific action, where appropriate, and recognized that some other concerns were exaggerated, your anxiety about your forthcoming holiday should be down to the level of pleasurable anticipation.

---

### Foreign travel

Let us apply the principles that we have already used for other internal obstacles to our pleasure and performance. The first thing to do is to raise our awareness of what is going on. This means listing all the concerns, however small, that we have. Do this on a sheet divided into four columns as shown below, then fill in the other columns.

| Concern | Situation | Action | By date |
|---|---|---|---|
| I won't be able to communicate | I do not speak French | Attend French language course | 1 July |
| The children will get sick | They are healthy now | Follow motor club scheme | 5 July |
| Hotel rooms inadequate | Cheap hotel | Switch hotel | Today |

## On the way

As soon as the journey begins you will probably indulge in a few 'if onlys'. You know the ones: 'If only I had a new car. . . If only we were rich and were going to stay in the Imperial Hotel in Monte Carlo instead of Pension Dubois in Paris. . . If only I – or my companion – was 15 years younger or 50 pounds lighter. . . If only my riotous kids were more like brother George's little angels. . . ' The fact is you are what you are, you have what you have, and you have done the preparation that you have done.

There is nothing you can do now about the special sun cream that you left on the bathroom shelf, so you might as well forget about it. On the other hand, if your anxiety about whether you left the gas oven on is driving you to drink, for heaven's sake phone your friendly neighbours as soon as you disembark, and do not carry the worry with you all the way to Paris. Mind you, finding a call box that works, and trying to figure out how to dial Little Bedrock from there may be the worse of the two evils, especially since there will be no reply anyway. Besides, you may have bigger things to worry about – like driving on the wrong side of the road.

## The wrong side of the road

In fact driving on the opposite side of the road is, even for first-timers, not nearly as difficult as people imagine, and foreign drivers are not nearly as fast or unpredictable as the lurid tales of earlier explorers might suggest. As I said, it is all in the mind, theirs and yours, and by adopting a relaxed attitude you adapt to the new conditions surprisingly quickly.

If you are an American driving in England for the first time you will probably find the transition more difficult, but that is because so many other things about driving in Europe are different too. Driving is far more regulated and prescribed in the United States, and the first impression for many Americans is that all European drivers are undisciplined, fast and dangerous. The fact that some Europeans do all this on the wrong side of the road is more than many an American is prepared to face. Since, as an American you are unlikely to bring your own car with you to Europe, you are also faced, in England, with rental cars having controls on the wrong side, and not only a stick shift, but one in the wrong hand!

When the English drive on the Continent, they face far fewer variables. Even if as a Briton you 'fly and drive' a left-hand drive car, you will find the car itself, the roads and the traffic behaviour throughout Europe very similar. In any case once you have driven the first few tentative miles on the 'wrong side', it soon becomes quite easy – provided you remain alert. The most common mistakes occur when restarting after a stop, or at a junction where there is little traffic about to remind you which side to go. Stop and think, or wait and observe and only drive on when you know what you are about.

## The law abroad

Many of us feel somehow immune from the law when we are driving abroad, and ignore speed limits and parking restrictions. Such behaviour is rude, dangerous and can be very expensive. It is a

◆ *Continental roads are full of surprises – some more dangerous than others...*

fallacy to believe that 'they cannot do anything to me because I am leaving the country tomorrow'. Increasingly Continental countries are demanding very high fines on the spot for speeding, and taking more confining action in serious cases. Pleading ignorance of the rules or pretending not to understand will get you nowhere, and rightly so. Ignorance is no excuse, and certainly no excuse for bad driving, wherever you are.

Every country has its particular driving peculiarities and special characteristics. Ultimately, certain rules, habits and characteristics should emerge as better than others, but it is a human failing to judge the way other cultures do things using your own way as the yardstick. If you drive through other countries constantly comparing their way unfavourably with yours, you will certainly have a frustrating time. It is far more useful to see how well you can blend your way of driving into the foreign traffic stream, and it is also likely to prove much safer.

What this does require, of course, is a greater degree of observation as you drive, and less reliance on assumption and expectation. It requires alertness and concentration of a high order, and the minimum of interference from your own anxious mind or from your passengers.

## Coping with bad conditions

List any other external conditions which increase your anxiety and tabulate the particular aspects of each that bother you. See if you are able to choose to do something concrete to reduce that concern; you may be able to ask another driver whom you trust to take you out in those conditions, or even go and practise on your own. Discovering that you are not a victim of circumstances will increase your confidence and abilities enormously.

## Distractions: passengers

We have looked at the elimination of flak from inside your own head, but to eliminate it from inside the car is probably impossible. Despite any amount of negotiation and agreement beforehand, motoring holidays abroad are certain to highlight differences between family members that did not appear to exist before. If this does not disturb the rhythm of the driver, the inevitable stream of requests for toilet and tea breaks surely will. Don't fight it; just accept the fact that everyone else's bladder is smaller than yours, and stop for them with a condescending air of extreme superiority.

If you drive smoothly enough maybe you can lull them off to sleep, or you could insist on playing your favourite tape as loud as you can stand. There are a limitless collection of games you can enrol them in, such as a competition for the largest total number of passengers seen travelling in VW minibuses in any given half hour!.

## Distractions: carphones

Carphones and CB radio are becoming so commonplace that I would be remiss if I did not comment on their effects on the driver.

Using a microphone or telephone occupies a hand which is better used for driving, and while it is no sweat to drive with one hand, two are undoubtedly better. Accordingly the official recommendation is that you stop if you wish to use the phone. The unavoidable fact is that most people won't stop, so if you have a carphone you need to learn to use it while on the move without letting it jeopardize safety. Once more, relaxed awareness of what you are doing is the secret. This will make you act more slowly and not overload yourself with activity as the road and traffic conditions vary.

Carphones and CB radios can actually be safety assets. CB helps many long-distance drivers overcome boredom and stay awake, as well as call for help when it is needed. Carphones can be valuable to business people and others who are held up in traffic, for they can phone ahead to explain why they are delayed and advise on their expected time of arrival. To be able to do so not only relieves the concern, which is an internal obstacle to safe driving, but it also means that the driver will not take the risks he or she might have otherwise been tempted to. Business people tend to get very irritated if they feel they are wasting their time, and sitting in a traffic jam is nothing if not a waste of time. To spend that time getting phone calls handled may pre-empt a frustration that is potentially more dangerous than the distraction of talking on the phone.

I expect that in a few years' time all cars will be supplied with 'hands free' carphones as routinely as the radio/cassette player of today. Who knows, you may be able to dial in someone's car registration number and tell the driver exactly what you think of his driving. But perhaps by then we will have transcended such nasty thoughts!

## SUMMARY

Even if we are confident that we can manage our internal obstacles under normal road conditions, anxiety is liable to creep back in if the weather is bad or we are driving unfamiliar cars in unfamiliar circumstances. There are other distractions too, such as passengers or carphones. By exploring some aspects of these unfamiliar circumstances the threat of the unknown is reduced, and the anxiety recedes.

# 5 Skill development

So far we have concentrated upon the steps needed to drive at our best under most conditions, most of the time. If you have been following the advice and trying it out on the road your driving ability will have undoubtedly improved because of your increased awareness and the reduction of your internal interferences. Now it is time to consider the refinement of existing skills and the development of new ones, but in order to do so we need to understand something more about the process of learning.

It is usually assumed that we learn best by being told, often in some technical detail, how to do something. Because of this assumption, many of us did not have a wonderful time at school, and sometimes find learning slow and unpleasant today. As teachers or parents, we easily slip into spouting our knowledge, giving little attention to how it is being received, assimilated and employed on the other end. Quite often it bounces straight off, and I believe that learning takes place in spite of such efforts, not because of them. So how do people learn? It is said that we learn more between our birth and our fifth birthday than we do in the whole of the rest of our lives. As the father of a boy who has just turned five, I do not dispute that assertion. Is it just coincidence, or is it an indictment of our school system that school starts at five?

I have watched my son acquire many new skills in his short life and I have taught him very little, in a conventional sense. He has picked up most of his intellectual knowledge by listening to adult conversation and by asking questions. He has learned most of what he can do from observing and experimenting. He has learned everything he has wanted to learn very quickly, and he has learned almost nothing that he did not want to learn. The faculties he seems to employ most are intention, observation and concentration. Above all, he enjoys himself.

If I was to teach a complete beginner to play golf, I would not tell him the Seven Golden Rules of golf on the way to the tee on the driving range. I would not even tell him how to hold a golf club 'correctly'. To do so would confuse him, it would suggest that golf is very difficult, it would overwhelm his memory and make him feel inadequate if he failed to remember all the rules, it would make him feel more dependent on me as an authority and it would consequently make him feel inferior. In other words, to do so would cause him to develop a number of internal obstacles which would prevent him hitting the ball effectively.

How much better it would be if I were to give him a bunch of golf balls and tell him to have a go, to have fun and to not care about the result. I would want him to satisfy his initial curiosity, to begin to get the feel of it and to enjoy experimenting with a new experience, before intervening with any kind of teaching process.

Unfortunately, we cannot do that in driving for obvious safety reasons, unless we have access to several square miles of concrete and a car with an indestructible engine and gearbox. Nevertheless, experimentation will certainly be the most effective way to develop the driving refinements you seek. I will give some hints and point you in a number of directions that I feel are worthy of exploration in the light of my own racing and driving experience, and from my observation of other racing and road drivers, but they are not the right or the only way. You will find your own best way as your experience grows.

There are, however, plenty of drivers who have driven huge mileages in their line of work, but are

*Skill development takes practice: the author in a 130 mph drift while testing a prototype Ford GT40 at Goodwood in the winter of '64.*

neither very safe nor very comfortable to ride with. The fact that they have, in their own opinion, 'never had an accident that was not the other driver's fault' means nothing. They have had a lot of experience, but they have not learned very much. Why not?

Experience alone is not enough. It is easy to become very experienced at repeating the same mistakes. We have dwelt at some length already on the importance of goals, motivation and awareness in every aspect of improving performance. To them we now need to add the observation and emulation of experts. Not only does this help us to define our goals more clearly but it will also instigate change at a more subconscious level. Once again we are back to those two fundamental questions: 'What do you want?' and 'What is happening now?'

## Observation for emulation

In order to know what you want, it is essential to have some kind of ideal. There are several ways to develop that, but observation of an expert is certainly one of the best.

Whenever you have the opportunity to ride with a good, experienced driver, use it by watching what he does, how he sits, how he moves his feet and hands on the controls, and where he places his attention. Then note all the external things like how he places the car on the road in relation both to other cars and to the changing road geography and conditions. Notice the smoothness of the ride, particularly during gear-changing, braking and cornering, and notice the sound of the engine.

By doing this you will acquire a set of standards, certainly, but more importantly your driving will automatically begin to move towards that standard, without you consciously trying to copy the expert. This may seem far-fetched, but it's not. For example, it is well-known that the standard of tennis on public courts in Britain improves dramatically for a week or two after the annual Wimbledon tournament has been filling the TV screens. All that mindless sitting in front of the box can have some benefit after all!

It follows, therefore, that riding frequently with bad drivers will not help your driving. Even though you may be very aware of the mistakes they are making, you will have a tendency to take some of them on board.

Ex-World Champion racing driver Jackie Stewart is a fine road driver. In conjunction with the Ford Motor Company, he runs a number of advanced driving days for specialist groups such as motoring journalists. Participants are able to ride with Jackie around a racetrack at fairly high speed in a normal road car while he explains what he is doing. It is a polished demonstration of good driving at its very best from which many already competent drivers, including myself, have benefited. Unfortunately, we cannot all get to ride with Jackie but, if you will admit it, you probably know drivers who are better than you. Ride with them. Soon you will have built up a store of good examples to aspire to, and you will already be improving. You will probably also find that you have more motivation to improve.

## Formula finesse

Aside from riding with Jackie, participants on these advanced driving days have the opportunity to try their hand at a smoothness exercise.

A car is equipped with a 'ball in a saucer' laid on the bonnet as shown in the photograph. The object of the competition is to drive a set number of laps as fast as you can over a small circuit marked out with plastic cones – without allowing the ball to roll out of the saucer. In what has now become the motor racing tradition, Moet and Chandon supply champagne prizes for the fastest times of the day but the champagne is seldom wasted as it is after a Grand Prix!

Obviously the purpose of this game is to cultivate smooth driving free from jerky changes in speed and direction. It may surprise some people to discover that in order to be fast, a racing driver needs to drive extremely smoothly. This is because in a race he is nearly always driving at the limit of adhesion between the tyres and the track. Any untidiness will cause the delicately balanced car to slide off the track or lose time. For this reason successful racing drivers are invariably good road drivers, and normally drive with the smooth efficiency of an experienced chauffeur.

◆ *Jackie Stewart (in dark glasses) briefs a group of motoring journalists on the finer points of his Formula Finesse 'ball in a saucer' test of smooth driving.*

## Other road users

If smoothness is the key quality of a good driver inside the car, then courtesy to other road users is the most important factor outside it. Other road users include pedestrians, who not only have rights, but who deserve our consideration too. We tend to forget that we are all pedestrians some of the time, and I have to admit that until I had a child to be an example to, I was not a good one. But this does raise an interesting issue.

Pedestrians, by and large, are polite to one another, and even quick to apologize if they accidentally interrupt another's path. Similarly the majority of people will hold a door open for others, or offer to let them through first, at least until the crowd reaches critical density. Then it is every man for himself, and to hell with the women and children. Even when push comes to shove, however, most people are content to manoeuvre in silence or mutter quietly to themselves.

## The ball in the saucer game

The home version of Jackie Stewart's exercise is to use a small saucer with a marble in it, and place it on the floor of the passenger compartment. The flatness of the saucer and the weight and size of the ball can be varied to alter the difficulty of the exercise. It should be sensitive enough to pop out if you make a rough gear-change, or even if you fail to ease off the brake just before you stop at the traffic lights, which I am sure you all do!

Another version of this is simply to put a glass of water in the passenger footwell. I am sure none of you would cause the glass to fall over on your drive to work, but do it each day for a while, and see if you can learn to spill less and less water. Once you have become familiar with the approximate loading that causes the water to spill, the trick is not to watch it, or even check how you are doing, until you get to work. This not only keeps your concentration on the road where it should be, but it teaches you to *feel* smoothness, which is how you learn to drive smoothly.

Finally when you think you are really good at this, try it with a glass full of indelible ink! This will give you a great demonstration of the tension that grips your body when mental or internal obstacles interfere!

Equip these relatively calm pedestrians with cars and many of them will mouth oaths and gesticulate rudely at anyone who holds them up or bruises their ego by passing them. When people are one step removed from the possibility of physical and verbal confrontation by being clad in automotive armour, they become more audacious and assertive.

But the causes of aggression among drivers may not always be so simple. Some authorities advocate the concept of 'defensive driving' as a means of ensuring that drivers are prepared for

➡ *Heavy traffic: 'relatively calm pedestrians' negotiating a contra-flow system on a city street.*

any potential danger. Its effect, however, if widely adopted by drivers, would probably be quite detrimental. A defensive attitude assumes an aggressor and evokes fear. Fear often produces unconscious aggressive behaviour, so defensive driving is transmuted into aggressive driving.

We have all come across that character who, constantly and with never a glance to the side, moves up abruptly very close behind the car in front just in case anyone should attempt to enter the traffic stream in front of him. He uses the bus lanes flagrantly but asserts his rights adamantly should anyone else do anything similar. He scowls and curses at anyone who might even be in a position to hinder him.

I sometimes wonder if he has a hell of a life or a hell of a wife, but I suspect that if one were to remove him from his car, he would turn out to be a mouse, or even a nice polite person like you and me. Although I must admit that I was one of them; well, not quite. I generally would let people in because it made me feel good, but God help anyone who pushed in uninvited. I would wave and shout like the worst of them.

All that came to an end one wet afternoon in East India Dock Road in London some 15 years ago. A taxi suddenly pulled out into my path and very nearly caused an accident. Our vehicles stopped inches apart. I jumped out and roared at him in righteous indignation. He waited until I had run out of breath and said very calmly and sincerely, 'I am very sorry, mate, but haven't you ever made a mistake?' His unexpected yielding at my aggression completely disarmed me – or was it just that I had become more vulnerable by getting out of my car?

I have been much more tolerant ever since, and when I have on occasion become the object of someone's wrath, I have used those same words which never fail to defuse the situation. We do all make mistakes at times and I believe that most of us really would like to be considerate to others on the road. My ideal is that there should be no limits to consideration, but I admit that at times I fall far short of that ideal. I find it helps a lot to view traffic movement, especially where traffic is heavy, as a flow; my job is to move in and out of that flow causing the minimum of perturbation. This way the progress of everyone is to my benefit. If I view it as a competition I will inevitably upset others, as well as myself, and there is nothing to win anyway. By disrupting the flow with my aggressive intrusions I actually slow it down, and I may lose more time than I gain.

If you adopt this attitude of maintaining the flow, things like road positioning, when and where to signal, when to yield and when to close up all become rather obvious. There is a collective purpose, a mutual venture in which other road users become unwitting partners, and co-operation is the game.

In line with that objective, I will always try to drive up to the speed limit, move sharply away from traffic lights in order that the maximum number of cars can get over behind me, and adjust my speed so as not to cause a line of traffic to build up behind me.

As a motorcyclist myself, I try to watch for motorcycles moving up between the lines of traffic and give them room to get by. I will try to keep rolling at road junctions and especially when joining a motorway; likewise I will always allow others in, even the pushy ones, so we all dovetail together. I always allow a car or two out from a side road into the main stream in front of me and always give way to a bus pulling away from a bus stop.

In the country I continually adjust my speed according to the road configuration and other vehicles by watching a long way ahead, thereby almost entirely eliminating the need to use the brakes. I try to make my intentions abundantly clear to other road users by being consistent in

➡ *If you learn how to blend with the flow...*

terms of speed and positioning and giving clear signals, which are not always limited to those in the Highway Code.

I do not consider any of this to be particularly virtuous, generous or clever on my part, nor does it require any particular effort. This is simply a compilation of some of the little things that I do automatically to help the flow and to maintain my own mental equilibrium when I drive. I only mention them because, in discussion with others, I have been amazed to find that so few average drivers think about them at all. What I have mentioned is a very incomplete list but I hope it will encourage others to see what adjustments they can make to their driving to make it work better for themselves and for others.

We are often exhorted to drive courteously. This does not mean we should adopt a mechanistic set of prescribed behaviours; what it does mean is that we should view other road users as worthy of kindness and consideration. The appropriate road behaviour for every circumstance will arise naturally out of that fundamental attitude. Of course there are occasions when, because we are in a hurry, or because some hooligan deliberately cuts us up, we all fall short of our ideals, but that should not undermine the courtesy principle.

*...you may even* enjoy *the traffic!* ➨

## Symbolic imagery

In the exercise at the beginning of this book you explored the qualities of the ideal driver you would like to be, but qualities can also be expressed in terms of symbols. For example, to you, a racing driver might symbolize calm, smooth, precise and fast driving; on the other hand an expert taxi driver might symbolize patience, and city street and traffic expertise. You can create your own symbols such as the courteous driver, the chauffeur, the economy expert, or the unobtrusive driver who can slip in and out of the traffic stream unnoticed, which is one I particularly like.

The way to use the symbols is to drive as if you were that symbol. Imagine you are a chauffeur, and drive that way. It is not so much a question of acting the role, but of adopting the feelings and the attitudes that such a person would have as they drive. It is a lot of fun doing it; it certainly prevents boredom, it provides you with new choices and it helps you to develop the qualities of your chosen symbol.

Be realistic, however; it is no good imagining you are the Red Baron in an open vintage Bentley, because when you get stuck in the traffic in Commercial Road you will get very frustrated.

It is tempting to list the negative counterparts to your ideal, and great fun and quite revealing playing the game, but I would not recommend it on the road. When I teach skiing, which I do whenever I get the chance, many people find it helpful if I get them to ski in different roles, and these may include being the beginner or the nervous skier. It helps them to break out of their stereotypes, to release tension and to lighten up.

Of course these games should not be taken to extremes. For example, the economy expert would make sure his engine is well tuned and his tyre pressures up to the mark; he might experiment with different routes, but mainly he would be concerned with what he does inside the car and how he flows with the traffic. I knew one person, however, who removed the back seat, radio and spare wheel for lightness, drove in bare feet for sensitivity, blew his tyres up to 55 psi to minimize rolling resistance, conserved energy by never using the heater, drove at a constant 30 mph and rarely stopped, even at traffic lights. He was going a bit far, but he did record 55 mpg and he thoroughly enjoyed his driving.

---

### Roleplay

Next time you are in your car, imagine you are the driver that best embodies the qualities you would like to develop. Don't *try* to drive with those qualities, just imagine what it would be like to drive with an abundance of those qualities. See if you can maintain this image throughout your journey, and notice the impact so doing has upon your driving.

---

## Information gathering

In order to drive smoothly, safely and with consideration for others, you need to gather and make use of as much relevant information as possible about your surroundings at every moment. For driving, sight is obviously the most important sense, but you should not underestimate how much your other senses contribute to the full picture. It is not uncommon to know something, and yet be quite unaware of how one got to know it. This knowledge was probably acquired by a sense other than sight, but the conscious memory did not record the experience. For example, you might be quite unaware of a momentary, miniscule loss of rear wheel adhesion and yet find yourself looking more closely at the road surface to try and see whether frost is forming.

### Touch and body sensations
I discussed earlier how feeling your hands on the wheel and your feet on the pedals helps you to operate those controls more smoothly and sensitively. You also use your body as a sensor through which you gather much vital information.

The steering wheel will tell you a lot about the road surface and the adhesion of the tyres. To an expert driver, the feeling through the steering wheel can also indicate if the tyre pressures are uneven, too soft or too hard. It can even indicate whether the steering geometry is correctly aligned, whether the wheels are balanced or whether the kingpins are getting worn. Likewise the brake pedal can reveal information about the road surface, the condition of the brake pads or whether the brake fluid is free of air bubbles. Some of these indications will be felt through the hands, the feet and the seat all at the same time, and you can interpret the combined feelings to make the correct diagnosis.

I will not attempt to describe, even in general terms, all the different sensations and what they mean. Apart from the fact that there are far too many combinations, words are too subject to individual interpretation for my descriptions to be of much value to anyone reading this book. The point that I want to make is that there is an infinite amount of information, of real significance to your driving, that is available; the more sensitive to it you are, the better driver you will be.

### Hearing
Most people involved in a specialized activity quickly develop extraordinary sensitivity, at least in the area of their expertise. Racing drivers are inherently no more sensitive than anyone else, but some, such as Jackie Stewart, show uncanny qualities.

I well remember the day I accompanied Jackie to Silverstone where he was to test the Formula One Matra. He was constantly lapping the 140 mph circuit a few tenths of a second under the lap record, when he came into the pits to complain of a slight tinkling sound from the left rear of the car under heavy acceleration. It was eventually traced to a small clip used to attach a single wire to a tube which had worked loose. One has to marvel at the supernormal hearing which enabled Jackie to pick out such a tiny sound from the earth-shaking roar of a 600 horsepower engine barely a foot from the back of his head.

As a racing driver, I too use my hearing a lot when I drive. Paradoxically my hearing has been permanently impaired by racing engine noise, and although I cannot hear the tick of a traffic indicator warning, I can hear minute changes in engine sound. While I can recommend the radio or cassette player to others for relaxation, I personally prefer to listen to the sound of the engine as I drive, and also the sounds of other vehicles. They can all give me vital information in addition to what I can see.

## Smell

I guess we can ignore the sense of taste when we drive, but an acute sense of smell can be an asset to a driver as an early warning of something overheating. A boiling radiator, hot engine oil on an exhaust pipe, brake fluid leaking onto a hot disc brake, an electrical fire and tyre smoke each have their distinctive smell, instantly recognizable to any competition driver. Whereas most road users don't have to contend with such things often, noticing such early warnings of a problem can save a great deal of money.

## Sight

And so we come to eyesight, the predominant sense for driving. First-class distance sight, with or without glasses, is a great asset, but a lot of people who can see well simply don't see enough. Some people look but they don't see, as in the classic excuse 'I looked both ways, but I did not see him coming'. Some people look at the wrong things, ranging from their passenger's gorgeous eyes to the back of the car in front. Some people see well, but interpret what they see poorly. Some people don't look at all.

To be aware means to receive regularly and clearly a broad range of input, and to understand the implications of that input. What is important in the visual context is the ability to scan automatically over the road ahead, other vehicles and people in the vicinity, other indicators that may be some distance from the road, as well as the mirrors and the instruments. A common fault is the failure to scan far enough ahead.

◆ *There's more to good driving than simply watching the road...*

## Scanning ahead

Next time you drive, check at regular intervals how far ahead you are looking, in yards or metres or using some other consistent criterion such as the next three cars in front. Do not try to change it yet. Notice exactly where you look under a variety of different driving conditions. If you find it changing for the better, let it, but do not force it.

After a few days, when you have become clear about what you do, begin to consciously look further ahead and notice the effect this has. Experiment with looking as far down the road as you can see, all the time. You will gradually gain confidence in your peripheral vision, which is well able to give you the input necessary to respond quickly to the pedestrian who unexpectedly steps off the pavement close by. You will need to keep monitoring where you look for several weeks, for you may have a persistent habit to break.

Looking only at the back of the vehicle in front is a related, and very dangerous fault. It results in parroting the driver in front, failing to anticipate changes in speed and direction, and ultimately in multiple motorway pile-ups. It may even lead to a driver stopping merely because the driver of the vehicle in front stops to post a letter!

There are many ways to remain aware of what is going on beyond the vehicle in front. You can look round either side of a truck as the road curves, or through the rear window if it is a car. The houses, trees or telegraph poles beside the road also indicate bends in the road, and the speed of the oncoming traffic will tell you if there is a clear road, an obstruction or a sharp turn just ahead. Most of all it is essential to keep easing out sufficiently to see ahead. This enables you to overtake as soon as possible if necessary. I rarely remain for long behind a truck, for safety's sake.

An expert driver will not have to keep checking each of these memorized indicators but will merely monitor them all automatically, cross-reference them, continually draw conclusions and then check the conclusions against reality. This will be a continuous, automatic and largely unconscious activity.

Until I started writing this book, I was singularly unaware of how I gather all the information that I act upon when I drive. More recently I have begun to check back to see what the indicators were. While driving for some time on a twisty alpine road between head-high vertical snowbanks, I noticed that I was anticipating the arrival, and even the size, of oncoming vehicles

➡ *Scan ahead! Keeping your eyes fixed on the back of the vehicle in front can be fatal.*

just before they came into sight. I realized that, even on a dull day, I was picking up the subtlest shadows thrown ahead of them onto the snowbanks as they approached. It was useful information.

Here is some more. Have you ever noticed that darker patches in the centre of the traffic lanes indicate where the bumps or undulations are, and even their severity? The reason for this is that as vehicles hit the bumps, the oil drips that accumulate underneath are thrown off to form stains on the road. Through this observation, it is possible to anticipate and minimize bumps by adjusting your speed accordingly. Eventually it will become second nature.

### Constant awareness

Constantly taking all this kind of information into account and automatically responding to it is the hallmark of an aware driver. There is no way I could list or you could learn all the subtle indicators, for there are hundreds of new ones every day.

The trick is just to remain aware as you drive. This may be hard to grasp, but it is worth repeating that it is possible for your unconscious mind to be reading and processing all the subtle signs, even though you are not recording them in your conscious memory. This may help you understand how it is quite natural to listen to music with your conscious mind for relaxation while still driving well automatically.

### Sixth sense

Any discussion of the senses would be incomplete without mentioning the sixth sense. I would be the last to deny the possibility of picking up information psychically or through one's intuition, but this may not always be the best explanation when you 'just knew something'.

When our awareness is well developed, we are drinking in a lot of information; some of this is minute and extremely subtle, but a variety of minute signs indicating the same thing will pass a strong message. Often we get the message but we don't see the messenger, and some may attribute this incorrectly to their psychic powers. But what is psychic power, if it is not a higher order of awareness?

---

### Reading the signs

As you drive, give yourself, or a tolerant passenger, a running commentary about all the indicators that you are using and what adjustment you make to your driving as a result of them. This exercise is known as an awareness continuum. If you do this for a few minutes on every journey, it will soon occur effortlessly, then automatically. The enhanced awareness you develop this way will make you drive more smoothly, and may even prevent an accident some day.

---

### Passive awareness

While you are driving, begin to notice how you are noticing, observe yourself observing, become aware of yourself being aware. In this chapter we have been mainly discussing the use of external indicators, but for the purpose of this exercise, add in your awareness of your own thoughts and emotions. Notice if you become frustrated on the journey, and if so, with what. Notice how your mind flits from subject to subject with apparent randomness. When it settles for a moment on your driving, what does it most often think?

This is not nearly as exhausting as you might expect; in fact if it is exhausting you, you are doing it wrong! It is tiring to scurry around your senses like a squirrel collecting a store of information and to be afraid that you are missing something, but that is not what I am getting at. Awareness is a calm, passive receptive state which needs some practice, but it soon becomes effortless. And the benefits are incalculable.

## Knowing your car

If you walk through a crowded supermarket or down a crowded high street you are most unlikely to bump into anyone else, even with a big shopping bag in your hand. Likewise a good tennis or squash player can swing a racket within an inch of a wall without hitting it, or worrying about hitting it. An expert skier's skis become an extension of his feet and he no longer has to keep looking to know where they are. When one reaches a fairly proficient level in any activity the tools of the trade become an extension of one's body.

When this condition begins to arise for a driver, and unfortunately it never does for some, he will experience a whole new level of skill. He will seldom again be concerned about where the corners of his car are, or how wide it is.

### How wide is your car?

In a friendly farmer's field or some similar place, stick two light canes into the ground, leaving a gap between them that you imagine you could just pass through in your car. Drive between them slowly. Do it again a little faster. Then set them again, with the car to measure from, just three inches (8cm) wider than the car on each side, and drive through as fast as you can.

Practise this every couple of days until you can drive through regularly and comfortably at 20 mph with a two-inch (5cm) gap on each side. It won't take you long, and you will soon see how much more relaxed you become, particularly in heavy city traffic.

Of course you can do the same for the length of the car by driving or reversing up to within a couple of inches of a cane. Then you can place a cane in the ground and practise turning close to it on the corners. You will need a friend to tell you how close you were each time.

Once you have mastered this with your own car, you will be amazed how quickly you get used to the size of other cars.

## Skill development through awareness

So far I have concentrated heavily on what goes on in your head and body. That is where it all starts. Get that right and the rest of your driving won't go far wrong. The relationship between a mind free of anxiety, a body free of tension, a comfortable seating position, fluid hand and foot movements on the controls and smooth, safe, and considerate driving are surely self-evident.

There is, however, always room for improvement in technique. To ride with and observe an expert is the ideal way to become aware of new possibilities and ways to improve, but what if you happen to be the best road driver in the neighbourhood?

I would not offer you an analysis of the available techniques or a list of hints and tips from the experts. Instead, I invite you to try the following exercise to enhance your use of awareness as a means of skill development.

## Feeling your way

Observe yourself and what you do as you drive. Notice how you use the clutch and gear lever. Do you plan to do so or does it just happen? What are the indicators that you use to tell you when to change gear? How exactly do you move the gear lever? What part of your hand do you use? Can you feel the separate notches as you bring the lever out of one gear into neutral, and from neutral into the next gear? How far do your engine revs drop between upward gear changes? Listen to the engine during upward gear changes; what do you notice? Feel the clutch pedal: can you feel the point at which it engages and disengages?

Try moving the gear lever with two or three fingers only, lightly. Change gear with two separate movements, out of one gear, pause, into the next. See if you can change up by letting the engine revs drop to the level appropriate to the next gear, rather than letting them fall right away and come up again. Do this by sound. Experiment with changing directly from second to fourth gear, or from third to fifth, and back again.

On an empty road set yourself a constant speed, say 30 mph, and see if you can change gear smoothly in every combination between first and fifth by varying the engine speed but not the road speed. Experiment with changing down while climbing a steep hill by having the revs build to the level of the next gear down without a little drop first. And these are only a few suggestions; try to come up with as many again of your own.

### SUMMARY

In this chapter we looked at the process of natural learning, through awareness and by observation and emulation. The key to good driving is smoothness inside the car, and courtesy outside it. We looked at some of the driving behaviours that make a courteous driver. An expert uses all of his senses while driving to gather a vast array of information which is processed to make the drive as safe and comfortable as possible.

# 6 Emergencies

When you are faced with an emergency, what do you do? If you have time to think about how to react, it was not much of an emergency anyway. The real emergencies are already over by the time you can figure out what to do. You will respond to the emergency without thinking, but how appropriately you respond will depend upon how well you have assimilated the lessons of all your driving experiences in the past. The richer and the more wide-ranging those experiences are, the more resources you will have to call upon.

Experience over the limit on a skid pan, or close to it during a session at a racing school, will undoubtedly help to prepare you for emergencies. Such sessions have the advantage that you are usually very aware of what is happening at the time. The fear, boredom, disinterest, inattention, frustration and anger often associated with road driving all have the effect of closing down awareness and limiting learning. This is perhaps why there are so many bad drivers on the road who have many miles of experience – of being bad drivers.

## The Saint Peter Principle

A driver's choice of speed is determined by a related factor which now comes into play. It is similar to the Peter Principle. Peter points out that employees rise up the organization until they reach their level of incompetence, at which time promotion ceases. For example, in a garage the best mechanic becomes the service manager, and if he manages well promotion continues. But if he is not so good, he fails to rise further and remains pushing paper with limited skill while his considerable abilities as a mechanic are wasted.

In driving we tend to increase the speed at which we drive until we reach the speed at which a little insecurity begins to creep in. In other words we are driving up to our limit, and this is where we gain considerable experience, but we rightly rarely go beyond that. If we allow conditions or circumstances to push us beyond our normal individual limits, however, we are immediately on untried and therefore unsafe ground. Furthermore the conditions or circumstances themselves, such as rushing for a train, bad visibility in a downpour or whatever, are likely to cause distraction, tension and other internal interferences to good driving. These two factors conspire to make us into an accident looking for somewhere to happen, while St Peter fumbles with the lock!

How much safer we would be if we were all to drive at say 25 per cent inside our limit or our experience, rather than *at* the limit. Alternatively – though it comes to much the same thing – how helpful it would be if we all had some practice at driving over our normal limits so that when those circumstances arise, we are much better equipped to continue in safety. Clearly the road is not the place to practise such things, but for the average driver the alternatives are not obvious.

Nothing can beat the experience gained by being a professional rally or racing driver for a year or two. There are very few conditions that one might encounter on the road, even under the most extreme circumstances, that a rally or racing driver will not have had to cope with many times over. A burst tyre, a patch of oil or ice on the road, or even a steering failure will barely affect the flow of conversation from a competition driver. He will have experienced far worse at far higher speeds and not infrequently, in the course of competition.

Because I know a little bit about driving, I am sometimes obliged to listen to road drivers' horror stories. After a lengthy build-up about how they got to be in a hurry on this narrow road in Provence with mother-in-law in the back, the climax of the tale is that a front tyre burst. The rest of the story consists of the list of things that *nearly* happened, like they nearly crashed into a flock of sheep or into a field, or nearly turned over, or they were all nearly killed.

What in fact happened was that there was a bang and a pull on the wheel to the left which the driver counteracted reasonably well, and he managed to stop the car without much trauma except to his nerves. To him this incident may have been the most exciting moment in his holiday, but it was far from the near-death experience he described.

The problem with him, and so many others like him, is that he is so close to his limits when he drives that if something out of the ordinary happens, however small, he is thrown into near

panic. If he had had any lessons, or better still experience of what can go wrong, he would have probably coped with it easily without having to resort to the double brandy afterwards. We would not dream of letting pilots fly us around without training them on engine failure procedures, and this is done by simulating an engine failure. What about doing the same for situations that drivers may experience? A simulated tyre burst?

I know of many a driver who 'thought the car was going to turn over' when a sharp corner caught him by surprise and he had to wrench the steering wheel round causing the tyres to squeal. The car was nowhere near turning over in most cases. In fact any fool can drive a modern car with properly inflated tyres on a flat tarmac area at more than 100 mph and suddenly turn the steering to full lock without the car turning over. The front wheels will skid so that the car will not turn as sharply as the steering was turned, but the car will not turn over unless it hits something.

Modern cars are built to safely cope with the most extraordinary stupidity and abuse that only fools and competition drivers can deal out. Even if we do end up having accidents, the seat belts and crushproof car centre-sections do afford us a lot of protection. I am not by any means advocating the taking of risks, but some people's fears, which are themselves a cause of danger, can be greatly relieved by knowing the reality.

The fact that cars are much more controllable than most people believe, and drivers are much more able has been demonstrated by many people. Frenchman Jean Sunny once drove a normal saloon car for more than 50 miles balanced on two wheels. Dutch skid school expert Rob Slotemaker could spin a car through more than half a dozen complete revolutions on sheet ice and stop the spin to drive the car out in any direction required. Film stunt drivers like Bud Ekins, who drove for Steve McQueen in the film *Bullitt*, can perform prodigious feats in relative safety because they know what they are doing.

◀ *'...the abuse that only fools and competition drivers can deal out.'*

◀ *'...prodigious feats in relative safety...' The author on the Cortina bobsleigh run in 1964.*◟

In motor racing, too, the normal state of the car, other than on the straight bits, is in a slide or a drift. To a layman that means a skid, which he usually associates with those last few moments of prayer before the crash. But to an experienced racing driver this situation is not the knife-edge that it might appear to be. Controlling a drifting car does require skill, but the quick steering and throttle adjustments a driver may make during the drift are not to save his neck, but to save time.

I will give you some other examples in rather more detail. **Note that the following practices are not to be tried on the public road under any circumstances.**

Among the experiences you will hopefully never have, is that of jumping a car over a hump-back bridge by mistake. Some people, namely rally drivers do it on purpose, and become very skilful at it. The technique differs according to the flight pattern of the car. If it is nose heavy, a burst of power on take-off will keep the nose up, to avoid a vertical landing. If it is tail heavy, a dab on the brakes on take-off will keep the nose from lifting too much.

Many rally drivers further reduce the damaging force of the landing by throwing the car a little sideways on take-off. This has the effect of bringing one front wheel down first so the landing load is spread over a longer period as it touches down – one wheel at a time. If the hump is shielding the view of a sharp turn immediately after it, as was the perverse practice of the country road builders of yesteryear, it is better to arrive at it somewhat sideways than straight, even if it appears to be the wrong side. This may seem a complete nonsense unless you have watched a rally or two on television.

On rough, slippery or loose surfaces, the normal rally cornering technique is to swing the car the opposite way first and then fling it back the other way into the corner. This is to initiate the necessary slide and stabilize the roll of the car over the outside wheels during the turn. If the driver happens to have picked the right way for the bend

after the jump, he already has the car set up the way he wants it for the turn. If it was the wrong way, a flick of the wheel will send it back the other way, as in the normal rally cornering technique. Either of these choices are faster than changing direction from straight ahead, when the driver has to energize this pendulum-like action before he can turn.

How do top competition driver develop these skills? By precisely the same methods that we have been discussing in this book for improved road driving, but with far more intensity. The goal of winning generates huge motivation, and the great awareness and sensitivity which they develop allows them to make apparently risky experiments with some confidence. They do not get it from books. They get it from their own experience.

◆ *Competition cornering: a driver using the slide to negotiate a bend in the 1987 RAC Rally.*

As in all sports, the best technique is never static. It is constantly being developed to take advantage of the engineering improvements that are also constantly being developed. Although there is remarkable consistency in the general technique employed by top drivers, there are as many individual refinements of it as there are drivers.

Racing and rally drivers inevitably use all kinds of methods of car control in competition that would give the average driving test examiner heart failure. That may not be surprising, considering the speeds at which they travel and the road conditions over which they compete. But those same drivers – who are undoubtedly among the best in the world – frequently use practices, at normal speeds on public roads, that would still be unacceptable to our driving examiner.

Thankfully there are no absolute laws about the technique of road driving, but driving instructors, examiners and police driving schools have preferences and recommendations which are consistent with good practice. Their adoption is often essential to pass certain driving examinations, but nevertheless they should not be taken as the only, or even the best way for every driver to drive.

If an already competent driver seeks to develop his driving further, he will need to experiment to find the smoothest, safest and most efficient ways of conducting the car, ways that are particularly suited to his individual physical and mental make-up. This is likely to lead him to cross the boundaries of 'correct' driving school procedure. However, if you find yourself doing things which are at variance with normal practice, it is important to be sure that what you are doing is truly smoother, more efficient and at least as safe under all conditions as the 'correct' way. You need to be certain that it is not merely a lazy habit which you have developed and which could be unsafe under certain conditions.

To illustrate this point, I will give a couple of examples of things that I do, which fit into this category. I am not recommending that you adopt them, but they are things that have contributed to the refinement of my driving.

## Approaching a bend

When approaching a tight corner, it is common good practice to brake and select the correct gear for the safe speed for the bend, apply steering as required and gently accelerate away from the corner. It is a simple, logical, step-at-a-time sequence, that most people can manage without

too much trouble. In racing a driver saves time by performing two of these steps simultaneously, by the use of the well-known 'heel-and-toe' technique. This means that he applies the brakes with the ball of the right foot and, at the same time, blips the accelerator with the heel or side of the same foot to obtain the right engine speed for the lower gear before engaging it. It enables him to employ the maximum retardation available from both the brakes and the engine simultaneously.

On certain corners racing drivers will break one of the other golden rules of driving by turning into the corner before releasing the brakes. The idea here is to encourage the rear end of the car to start sliding. The driver is then braking, changing down and turning – all at the same time.

On the road I often use combinations of actions like this, not for speed but for smoothness. It is something that should be allowed to develop naturally, though. Forcing yourself to combine movements when you have had only limited experience of driving can easily lead to confusion, and an accident. They are certainly not unsafe practices, but if copied by unskilled drivers, some of them could be. They are therefore not recommended for the average driver.

Let us now take the example I have used a step further. In racing, where you need every bit of retardation you can get, on the open road before the advent of speed limits and disc brakes, or in order to pass your driving test, the approved sequence of events as first described is, or was, ideal. Engine braking takes some of the load off the brakes, and under some circumstances this can be very useful. Today's brakes are quite powerful enough, however, and they need no assistance from the engine, especially from a mere 70 mph.

For the smoothest ride and economy of movement in road use, I usually brake down to the required speed, remaining in top gear, and only skip directly to the appropriate gear at the moment I want to accelerate away, which may be not until the apex of the bend. This certainly would not be the thing to do on your driving test, or unless you are confident of being able to combine the actions naturally and without having to think

about them. Until then, it is sensible to first brake, then change down before you get to the corner – but don't make a rule of it!

## Steering

The starting, or straight ahead, position of the hands that most of us accept to be the best is about 'ten minutes to two', viewing the steering wheel as an imaginary clock. One long-established rule of driving forbids crossing your arms beyond the twelve and six position when turning the steering wheel for a bend. We are taught to pull and push the wheel from hand to hand, and straighten it again in the same way. This method is generally considered to provide the ordinary driver with balance and control combined with flexibility and safety.

In the past, when road surfaces were poor and the steering of the day transmitted the effect of every pebble to the hands of the driver, it was necessary to grip the wheel firmly with both hands whenever possible. Most cars were heavy to steer then, even though steering wheels were larger to provide more leverage. Equally important was the fact that the castor action, or self-centering effect of the steering varied enormously from car to car. This meant that the return to the centre position had to be positively controlled. Today, with improved road surfaces, smaller steering wheels and much lighter and more positive steering on our cars, this is arguably no longer so necessary, but it remains the practice recommended by the police and other official bodies such as the RAC, the AAA and the IAM, whose experts are usually ex-police instructors.

I personally do not adhere to this recommendation but if you wish to pass various official driving tests you will need to conform to it.

My experience in teaching sport indicates that our bodies are very good at discovering the most efficient and effective way to perform any task. The more confident people become in any activity, the more they trust their experience and naturally adopt the methods that are best for them. This is

what I believe many drivers do with steering technique, once they have passed the driving test.

I have spent a night or two as a passenger in a patrol car and experienced a few emergency calls. I am impressed by how well a person can drive using the push-and-pull technique, which to me, looks unnatural. Racing and rally drivers do not use the push-and-pull method today, either in competition or on the road. They will, when necessary, pass the twelve and six position and may let the castor effect straighten the wheel after a bend by letting the wheel slip through the hands – but I must add that they *never* let go of the wheel altogether.

The British police did, however, recognize the expertise of competitors when, in the mid-thirties, they invited two top racing drivers of the time to establish the correct driving technique for all police drivers. Sir Malcolm Campbell and Lord Cottenham did their job well, and passed on the state of the art as it stood then, within the limitations of car design that I have already mentioned. Given the huge changes in steering technology in the past 50 years, it is perhaps time for the police to recheck with the advisors that they trusted before to set their standards. My

*Skilled drivers can slide cars with confidence. Here the author in Stirling Moss's Lotus (car 90) is fighting for the lead with car 91, and both are about to lap the cars in front.*

hunch is that a consortium of today's top competition drivers would suggest a number of changes in the techniques they use, and in the recommendations they make to other drivers.

## Supersensitivity

The ability to feel what is right is an attribute which top performers in every field develop because of the need to extract the utmost from themselves and their equipment. This applies both to the techniques they employ, and to the development of the tools of their trade.

Top tennis players keep a battery of tennis rackets strung to different tensions, and select the one they deem appropriate to the circumstances. At my level of tennis, any old racket will do, and I could not tell the difference anyway. Competitive skiers experiment with endless variations of skis and wax to make them as fast as possible in snow which is never the same twice. Most recreational skiers are satisfied to rent whatever the ski shop has available.

Competition drivers are sensitive to all manner of tiny details about their vehicles that are beyond the comprehension of other drivers, even if driving is their primary occupation. By driving a production road car at its limits round a race track, a racing driver can discover and identify flaws in a car's feel and handling that few manufacturer's test drivers would ever notice. In normal road use such details do not show up as dangerous faults, but a car owner may notice, for example, that this particular model feels a little less secure than other cars he has owned, or that he feels a little more tired than usual after a long journey.

Motor manufacturers were sceptical at first, but now they are recognizing that this skill possessed by racing drivers can be a great asset when designing new cars. Jackie Stewart, for example, has been involved in the development of Ford's new models for years.

Most manufacturers have at one time or another run a works rally team both for publicity and for its development value. Such programmes have resulted in all road cars having huge built-in safety margins. Knowing and appreciating this should reassure those drivers who are afraid of what their cars might do to them. Of course, telling a driver about a car's inherent stability and its controllability in extreme circumstances is no substitute for actual experience of what happens at the limit. There is, of course, no short cut or totally safe route to that kind of experience, and few people would volunteer for it anyway, but there is a partial substitute. One or two lessons on a skid pan at a high-performance driving school, or a day spent at a reputable racing drivers' school, may be expensive but it would probably make you a safer and more confident road driver for the rest of your life.

I expect and hope that driving schools of the future will have off-the-road practice areas or aircraft-type driving simulators for many purposes but particularly to provide experience beyond the normal limits. This way, people's day-to-day driving would be well within their own capabilities. I am sure there are readers who have spent an hour or two driving at high speed on German autobahns, after which a mere 70 mph seems easy. This is a taste of the cushion of confidence that an expert driver feels all the time. I wish I knew how to convey it to everyone.

## SUMMARY

Limitations in training opportunities mean that most drivers are poorly prepared, mentally and in terms of skill, to cope with the emergencies that are bound to arise from time to time.

Competition drivers, on the other hand, are so familiar with driving close to the limit that they are confident and efficient in situations far more extreme than are likely to be encountered on the road.

Skid pan and racing school lessons are recommended to those road drivers who wish to develop their skill, safety and confidence.

# 7 What car?

So you have explored your driving to the limit. By now you should have a greater understanding of your driving as it is now, and about your ideal and your potential to become an expert. We are back to those two questions 'What is happening now?' and 'What do you want?' Your driving will have already begun to improve as long as you have not sabotaged the natural learning process by trying too hard.

You have probably also become more interested in the various technological advances and options that motor manufacturers are making available, and you are certainly in a better position to appreciate them. So let's have a look at the advantages and disadvantages of the most important ones, and how to make use of them.

## Automatic gearbox
A lot of Europeans have never driven a car with automatic transmission, and a lot of Americans have never driven one without. Despite this I shall assume that all readers of this book know the basics of both systems and I shall simply point out a few refinements of technique.

Most automatics have provision for the driver to hold the lower gears manually when required, such as on a steep hill or to obtain maximum acceleration from low speed. Changing up or down either automatically or manually normally entails a slight lag and/or jerk but this can be virtually eliminated by subtle use of the throttle. I will not attempt to describe this for it can only be discovered by feel, and each type of gearbox is slightly different.

There is a controversy surrounding automatics and that concerns the 'correct' use of the feet. Do you use the right foot on both the accelerator and the brake, or do you use one foot on each? I combine the two, generally using the right foot only on the open road but both feet in town or in heavy traffic. I can stop, start and crawl along in traffic more smoothly when I use both feet. The argument against using both is that most drivers are used to pushing a clutch with the left foot which is a

➤ *The great foot controversy: should you use one foot to control both throttle (left) and brake (centre), or one foot on each (right)?*

sharper movement. Until a driver gets used to using his left foot more progressively, he may well throw his passenger and even himself into the windscreen, in which case he will learn very quickly!

Some drivers, who consider themselves to be experts, are disparaging about automatics, but they have their uses. I am happy with automatics in most conditions and find them pleasantly lazy to use in town. I do not like them in snow and ice for they do not afford me the subtle control that I need. A good driver can always get a better performance in terms of speed, economy and even smoothness from a manual box.

### Diesel engines

At least one diesel-engined model is now offered by most major motor manufacturers. The benefits of diesel engines are their reliability, longevity, good fuel consumption and good pulling power in the middle range. Diesel fuel is also some fifteen per cent cheaper than petrol in Britain at present. Diesels are at their best covering high mileages on long journeys with heavy loads.

The commonly held view is that diesels suffer from more engine noise, roughness at low engine speed, and comparatively sluggish response and performance. But these areas are constantly being improved by manufacturers and the difference is now negligible. Another drawback is that diesel fuel is not always available at all filling stations and it is certainly more messy than petrol when refuelling. Finally in Arctic conditions even the heavy-duty batteries used may have difficulty turning over a high-compression diesel engine, and diesel fuel can 'jelly' in the tank. Despite all this I loved the diesel Mercedes I once owned.

### Front-wheel-drive

Early front-wheel-drive cars were notorious for their heavy steering and a considerable difference in their turning arc depending on whether the power was on or off. If power was applied in a turn, the car would tend to plough straight ahead, a behaviour known as understeer. Conversely if the

power was suddenly reduced in a turn, the car would tend to turn more sharply into the corner.

These tendencies have been all but eliminated by most manufacturers, to the degree that only the more skilled drivers can feel the difference between modern front- and rear-wheel-drive cars in normal conditions.

The only circumstance under which that difference really shows up is on slippery wet roads and on ice and snow. When adhesion is lost in a front-wheel-drive car, the steering effect and the transmission of power to the road are lost simultaneously. As the car slows, the front wheels take hold again, restoring the steering effect and allowing the power to be gently re-applied. It is simple and logical to control. The only thing to remember is not to turn the steering wheel more when the steering effect is lost. To do so will only delay the moment at which adhesion is regained, and when that happens the car may make a rather sudden turn in the direction the wheels are pointing at the time.

An inexperienced driver is likely to find a front-wheel-drive car marginally easier to control on slippery roads, and may therefore feel safer in one,

➡ *Apparently steering for the wall, the author demonstrates front-wheel-drive understeer in a racing Mini Cooper.*

which accounts for their early popularity. Manufacturers also prefer this layout for small cars when space is at a premium. Front-wheel-drive concentrates all the mechanicals at the front, leaving more luggage space at the rear. It also avoids the need for a central drive shaft tunnel protruding into the passenger compartment, and it has some weight and cost advantages.

## Rear-wheel-drive

In a rear-wheel-drive car, the steering and the power act more independently of one another, so there are more variables to play with. For many drivers, mastering a skid in a rear-wheel-drive car is a more satisfactory feeling, and off the public roads it can be fun. The front wheels may skid, but usually only owing to the momentum of the car and the application of too much steering.

Applying too much power in a bend on a slippery road is likely to cause the rear of the car to skid outwards. This is known as oversteer. The car seems to turn more sharply than the driver intended, and this can be corrected by winding off some steering. If the skid is prolonged or the

➡ *This rally car is steering to the right at the end of a left-hand hairpin, demonstrating the art of rear-wheel-drive oversteer.*

driver's response is too slow, the steering may need to be quickly turned all the way onto opposite lock to correct the skid. This is not nearly as difficult as it may sound; in fact it is an instinctive response. A more violent or uncorrected skid may result in a 180 degree spin, and the car will end up pointing backwards.

## Four-wheel-drive

Apart from all-terrain vehicles like jeeps and Land Rovers there are two main types of four-wheel-drive vehicle.

The first is similar to the jeep, having two-wheel-drive, either front or rear, for normal road conditions with the option of engaging four-wheel-drive. Most cars of this type also have a very low ratio four-wheel-drive selection available for particularly difficult conditions such as pulling trailers out of muddy fields. A good example is the Japanese Subaru.

The second system, as employed in the Audi Quattro and now on many cars, is a permanently engaged four-wheel-drive system with a sophisticated central differential to allow all the wheels to turn at different speeds, which they have to do in a turn. While also excellent 'down on the farm', these cars offer extraordinary sure-footedness under all road conditions. Because of the high cost of such systems, they are not widely available on smaller cars.

The handling characteristic of this type of four-wheel-drive car is that it is neutral, meaning that it has a good balance between the characteristics of front-wheel-drive and rear-wheel-drive, or between understeer and oversteer. This provides excellent skid prevention and easy recovery capability. Even on dry roads, where skidding should not be an issue at normal speeds, these cars are more pleasant to drive than their two-wheel-drive counterparts – and they use hardly any more fuel.

## Anti-lock braking systems

Available on their own, but almost always accompanying the sophisticated four-wheel drive systems, these devices stop the wheels locking under braking. Most drivers will lock their brakes during an emergency stop, but a car stops in a shorter distance if the wheels do not lock. Locking the front wheels also causes a total loss of steering effect. The system's strong point is that it improves stability in the brake and swerve manoeuvre so often needed in an emergency, wet or dry.

Usually electronically operated, the device releases the brakes the instant they lock and does so repeatedly in a very short time, maintaining maximum retardation without the driver having to make any adjustments to the pressure he applies to the brake pedal. It is a great asset to safety in all circumstances and outstanding on ice and snow. Its only drawbacks are its price and the fact that it may inspire overconfidence on ice where the stopping distances will always be greater than normal.

### Four-wheel steering

The next innovation, currently offered by one Japanese manufacturer and promised by others, is four-wheel steering. The technical arguments in favour of the system made by the manufacturer are impressive, particularly for low-speed manoeuvring. When I tried it, I found the steering very responsive at all speeds and the turning circle very tight, with a complete absence of tyre scrub. A more comprehensive road and track test might reveal some other advantages, or possibly defects, but so far I like it.

### Active ride suspension

Active ride suspension was pioneered by Lotus for Grand Prix racing cars, and it is under development by half a dozen major road car manufacturers. It could be the most exciting technological advance we have seen in years, for it promises to revolutionize the concept of a smooth ride on a rough road. It even has the capacity to reverse the direction of body roll on cornering and nosedive on braking.

It works by a system of on-board computers which monitor the suspension thousands of times per second and causes a compensation for every movement that is sensed. Those who have driven a

car so equipped claim that the smoothness of its ride is little short of miraculous, but lest you get too excited, it is some years away from going into production.

## Motives and priorities

In recent years the motor manufacturers have made remarkable progress in car design and there are undoubtedly more exciting innovations on the way. It is a pity that our ability to make use of these technological marvels is being eroded almost as fast by congestion and regulations. Fast cars have always been macho symbols, but at one time you were able to make full use of their performance too. Today, unless you are going to hire your own race track at weekends, the new 200 mph F40 Ferrari, and many lesser vehicles, are nothing but symbols – and rather impractical ones at that.

Motor manufacturers, like arms producers, have always been profitably responsive to man's desire for large ego-boosting projectiles, with only marginally more concern for the quality of life and

➡ *Who wants to carry passengers? The engine of this high-performance Renault occupies the space normally reserved for the back seat...*

the environmental impact they create. If we go on as we are, and we are not blown up by the other lot, we are liable to finish our days in a lethal polluting planetary traffic jam.

Mankind has an uncanny knack of averting disaster in the nick of time and I am an optimist, but I do believe that we all need to play our part in restoring sanity to our roads, at least. This means having some regard for the social and environmental effects of the cars we buy, and more concern for the skill and safety with which we use them. If some of us are still driven to proving our manhood in fast cars, let us find an arena other than the public roads on which to do it. Go motor racing, if you must. That is what I did, but a course of psychotherapy is a great deal cheaper!

## Accessories
Having bought a car you have to choose your accessories. You will need a radio to tell you to avoid the road you are on, lest you get stuck in the traffic jam you are in. Make that a quadraphonic cassette player to transport the mind, if not the body, out of it all. And you must have a carphone to tell them you are going to be late.

It is hard to avoid the hype. Accessory manufacturers and gadgeteers conspire with the promoters of plastic money to seduce us with all manner of instruments, devices, tools and fluids for needs that we never knew we had. Psychedelic stick-on graffiti, imitation fur seat covers and the ever-faithful dolly danglers are being phased out to make way for the car alarms to drive your

neighbours wild, and front spoilers and rear wings to keep you on the ground should you ever go over 130 mph. All these things are packaged to look like an essential bargain, but they lose their attraction after a week or two when the paint and the novelty wear off.

## Used cars
Have you considered buying a used car? Your choice for the money expands enormously if you do. However, if you thought the accessory business was confusing, this is a minefield through which I will leave others, more courageous and experienced than I, to wander. My personal view is that, within the limits of expected reliability, I would rather have a used car of the make and model that I want than a lesser car that is new, for the same price.

## Classic cars
One type of used car may be of particular interest to the enthusiast and the investor alike. There is already a flourishing market in cars built between 1945 and 1965, even rather mundane models. These are known as classic cars. It is probably both a reaction against galloping technology and planned obsolescence and an attempt to recapture the feel of driving in 'better' days. The prices of these cars are rising fast, spares are widely offered, several glossy classic car magazines are published regularly, and garages are springing up which specialize in restoring and selling particular models.

It is now possible to pay as much for a restored 1962 3.8 litre Jaguar saloon as you would pay for its brand-new, modern equivalent. Even replicas of classic cars are big business, and very expensive.

While some people choose to trade the safety, smoothness and silence of the current models for the nostalgia and the instability of a classic car, they will never recreate the open, unlimited roads that these cherished old cars enjoyed.

◀ *Fast and fancy it's not – but even a modest 'classic' car has style.*

## Motorcycles

A quick way to leave behind many of the frustrations of driving today is to shed a couple of wheels. More and more drivers are acquiring a motorcycle instead of a second car.

A motorcycle has been my primary form of transport ever since I moved to London ten years ago. It was immediately clear to me that the long and unpredictable car journey times, and the difficulties of parking, were going to constitute a massive and frustrating waste of valuable time. A motorcycle was the solution.

I can get anywhere in London from my home in less than half an hour on the motorcycle, regardless of the time of day. I am never late for appointments, parking is free and easy, and I never become irritated with the traffic. And the performance of a modern bike is tremendous. It sounds wonderful, doesn't it? But, as with all good things, there are some downsides.

No one can deny that the risk of accident and injury is high, and the motorcycle accident statistics make disturbing reading. A motorcyclist is very vulnerable, and a minor scrape in a car can be a major accident on a bike. A motorcycle is both

◆ *Motorcycles are fast through traffic, and fun to ride – but vulnerable.*

less visible, and less inherently stable than a car. Slippery roads affect a motorcycle's braking distances more than they do a car's, and metal manhole covers are lethal in the wet. If an emergency does arise a car driver has a better chance of avoiding accident and injury by a violent manoeuvre. Finally essential protective clothing – helmet, leathers and waterproofs – are tedious to struggle into and hot once you have, unless you move off immediately.

I have owned motorcycles ever since my teens, and I am experienced enough to be fairly confident of my ability to handle them under most circumstances. However, the unpredictability of a car driver who sees me too late, or not at all, remains a constant concern, and I never ride without lights on. Even if the drivers do see me coming, few pedestrians crossing between the traffic ever think to look out for a motorcycle.

I personally am willing to accept these risks, and to ride as responsibly as I can with them in mind, to gain the enormous benefits a motorcycle offers.

Quite apart from the practical advantage of motorcycles there is the sheer pleasure of riding them. They demand much more skill and finesse to use smoothly and well than cars do, so they are more interesting in daily use. For this reason, the exercises included in this book on relaxation and the use of controls are particularly relevant and easily adaptable to motorcycling.

Motorcycling today is more reminiscent of the heyday of open road motoring, and as such it generally provides a lot of pleasure to those who do it, something that is beyond the comprehension of those who don't. One cannot deny, however, that because of their noise, racy appearance, and the often dubious behaviour of their riders, motorcycles are only marginally less antisocial than smoking. The joys of motorcycling are not much appreciated by other road users.

➥ *Raw power, naked and unashamed: magic for some, hooliganism on wheels for others.*

## My own car

Being a social kind of fellow, I do also own a car. On weekdays my wife prefers to use public transport but we keep a car for occasional evening use, short weekend trips, the odd journey of 100 miles or more and an annual marathon down to the Alps for skiing. It is the economy model of a popular small car.

It is unpretentious; hardly worth stealing, in fact. The aerial pushes in so I do not have to use a wire coathanger and the radio pulls out so I am not forever picking granules of glass out of the floor mats. I live in one of those places described as a high crime area and, just to confirm it, my motorcycle was stolen from outside the house on the very day we moved in. Car alarms bleep all night outside, but nobody takes any notice.

Not long ago a friend came to dinner, and ended up staying the night. In the morning I realized that I should have warned him to leave his car elsewhere, since he was the type who has wall-to-wall sound in his car. He rushed out anxiously to see if all was well. His sound system was untouched but all four wheels had been stolen. The car was lying unceremoniously on its belly – but I digress.

Over the years our little car has collected a number of surface blemishes from being parked on this street, and borrowed by all and sundry, but I never worry about it. It is utterly undemanding, and has never let me down. I do no more than check the oil, battery and tyres, and run it through the Wash'n'Vac every couple of weeks. I take it to the nearest dealer for routine service at the correct intervals, normally once a year. It was delivered six years ago with no optional extras, and apart from the portable radio, it has acquired only one since – a baby seat!

It suits us perfectly. Of course it is slow. It is only capable of substantially exceeding the speed limit in very favourable conditions. With a roof rack and all my ski gear on top and the family inside it is embarrassingly slow, demanding the use of third gear on the slightest incline or against even a moderate headwind. Needless to say, I have never been stopped for speeding and I never even worry about the possibility.

It is an old familiar friend which has become an extension of me, and I get a surprising amount of pleasure from driving it. Because it is so slow, it requires considerable skill and ingenuity to get anywhere quickly, and I enjoy the challenge of using momentum instead of power to keep the speed up – and the fuel consumption down. I can drive it very smoothly indeed, and entirely effortlessly. This is the magic of driving to me, and since it has little to do with speed, it is available to me every time I climb into any car.

I enjoy the feeling of my hands flowing in slow motion over the controls. A continuous slow arm movement may combine a gear change with a flick of a switch and the initiation of a turn of the steering wheel; the turn is transferred to the other arm which takes over and completes it before flowing back to the neutral position. Two or three hundred horsepower underfoot may be exhilarating on the track, but on the road I prefer the sensuous feeling of flowing along a winding lane, an alpine pass or even among other traffic, relying on the contours of the road, the momentum of the car and the roll of the body to smooth out the changes in speed and direction.

In any case if the joy of driving is to you nothing less than dashing along the Riviera like James Bond in some exotic machine, you are destined to spend most of your motoring life disappointed and frustrated. If, on the other hand, you can discover the joy of driving on the local roads in your modest family car, your motoring life will be rich and rewarding. An expensive car is most unlikely to transform the inner state of its driver, and it is certainly not going to transform our overcrowded roads into the Garden of Eden or the old Nurburgring.

➥ *They look better in the showroom window than they do on the road...*

As a racing driver, I have been entrusted with many exotic road cars, and I have owned one or two myself. I have enjoyed them too, but it is not the ownership of cars that gives me pleasure, it is the skilful driving of them, and the attitude with which I drive. The joy of driving is a potential that we can all realize. It does not lie out there, elegantly sculptured in metal; it is inside each of us. Above all, it costs nothing. The secret is to enjoy what we have rather than to lust after something that we imagine we would enjoy more. It may demand a little patience, though, for it takes time to fully appreciate the finer points of what we already have.

Finally, what we drive and how we drive it reflects the way we are. It is obvious that a calmer attitude in life will result in calmer driving, but it is also true that if we change how we drive, we change a little bit of ourselves. If we learn to eliminate anxiety and frustration from our driving, we will have learned a way to eliminate them from other aspects of our life. If we learn the art of relaxed concentration as we drive, we may be able to apply it to our golf and our work life too. If we discover the joy of driving in the current driving climate, perhaps we will also be able to find a little more joy in the other imperfect circumstances of our daily lives.

---

## Acknowledgements

The list of all those who have assisted me along the road to the understanding from which this book stems would be a long one, but I make a special mention of the following: Alan Stacey and Bill Basson who helped me to get started on the right track; the late Jim Clark, and his fellow countryman Jackie Stewart who survived a long and dangerous career to make motor racing safer for everyone else, and to whom I am very grateful for writing the foreword to this little book. Their driving was exemplary and their friendship unfailing. My friend of many years, Miki Walleczek, who is the best road driver I know. Don Moore, Stirling Moss, Walter Hayes, Alan Mann, and more recently Peter Bryant who provided me with the breaks that I needed and helped to channel my exuberance into success on the track.

On the psychological side Bob Kriegel, Tim Gallwey, Graham Alexander, Alan Fine, David Hemery and a dozen less visible friends have all played their part in developing the mental skills described in these pages.

**Sir John Whitmore**